The Missing Rocks of Hampi

The Missing Rocks of Hampi

Mala Kumar

Illustrated by Megha Vishwanath

ink | OCCAM | yuva

ISBN: 978-93-6547-263-9

First published in India 2025
This edition published 2025

BluOne Ink Pvt. Ltd
A-76, 2nd Floor, Sector 136, Noida
Uttar Pradesh 201301
www.bluone.ink
publisher@bluone.ink

Printed and bound in India by Thomson Press (India) Ltd.

Kali and Occam are imprints of BluOne Ink

Director's Message YUVA Books

Dear Reader,

I'm glad you picked up this book. It means you're interested in Bharat's history, which is a good start. When we think of history, we often picture a list of endless dates, wars, and the struggle to remember the chronology of the governor generals of India—enough to put anyone off! I, too, did not enjoy history as a subject in school because of how it was taught. And sadly, not much has changed in the years that have followed.

We spoke to many children about this, and we got a standard answer: History is boring. This became a challenge for us. How could we make history interesting, inspiring, and exciting? How could we go beyond the insipid details of dates, chronologies, and dynasties to give it a breath of fresh air?

Indian history, right from colonial times, has been taught with a Western worldview. It has made us feel ashamed and apologetic about our past. We have been taught that certain dynasties or empires mattered more than others. We have been fed the central-regional divide without knowing what makes some histories central or regional.

While researching for my eighth book, *Bravehearts of Bharat: Vignettes from Indian History*, I grappled with these questions. So I tried to bring into the limelight those warriors and leaders whose stories were ignored or dismissed in the past as merely regional. This was also part of the vision that guided the creation of the Foundation for Indian Historical and Cultural Research (FIHCR)—an initiative dedicated to restoring our historical and cultural legacy and fostering pride in our past.

However, research alone is not enough. History must be told in a way that resonates, especially with young minds. This is where FIHCR YUVA comes in—to make history fun, engaging, and relevant.

YUVA goes beyond textbooks to present our past through a mix of storytelling, interactive maps, documentaries, and more.

At a recent talk, someone asked me, 'What is the point of all this? Why correct or unearth history?' While the answer to that is quite long, an important part of it is that it reaches the younger generation in a language that makes sense to them and that they can relate to.

When we began the journey of FIHCR in June 2024, YUVA was perhaps the only team without a set roadmap, because we wanted to hear what young people in India had to say. They said they wanted to learn history without pressure, told in a way that sparks curiosity and pride. So, dear reader, this book is our attempt at just that. The author, publisher, illustrator, and the entire FIHCR team have worked tirelessly to bring this book to life—the one that you now hold in your hands.

It is a pleasure to present *The Missing Rocks of Hampi* by Mala Kumar, a book that brings Hampi's breathtaking landscapes and mysteries to life. Through a captivating blend of history and storytelling, this book invites young readers to step into the world of this ancient city, uncover its secrets, and develop a deeper appreciation for India's heritage. I hope this book ignites curiosity about our past and makes history an adventure worth exploring.

Happy reading!

Warm regards,
Dr Vikram Sampath
Author/Historian/Fellow of the Royal Historical Society UK
Founder-Director, FIHCR

School Is Closed

This could not have happened! School has closed indefinitely? Devyani, pinch yourself, you're dreaming again. I did, and I was not dreaming. This was a nightmare.

'No school, no school, no-o-o-o schoo-oo-oo-l,' sang Sarang. Ever since Brigadier Jambu uncle from B-6 told my kid brother that he sings well, he has simply stopped talking. All he does is, sing. All. The. Time.

'Stop it, you silly fellow! Can you imagine being cooped up in the house all day?' Ugh! And listen to him sing all day long, I added in my head.

I turned to the TV as the screen filled up with all sorts of flashing graphs and figures. Five people spoke animatedly, each one trying to out-shout the other.

The anchor cut in smartly at one point. 'But Sir, why seal the school now? After all, there have been many companies working from Manhattan Towers since it came up five years ago. What was the department doing all these years?'

'Busy giving approvals for illegal buildings elsewhere!' shouted Amma, as though she were a part of the panel discussion. 'This building has no business coming up over a lake bed. What I can't understand is how a school with such a sane board of advisors could have agreed to move into this insane building!' Amma is well known in the city as Dr Brinda Ratnagar, a water management consultant.

Just a week ago, she was on a TV chat show with a young, violet-haired student researcher, a water board member, an environment lawyer, and a television anchor who kept sipping water from a glass with a bold sticker showing off a prominent drinking water company's logo! I had watched the show just because I felt it would somehow help me write an essay or do a school project; natural resources are a favourite with our teachers! These are the things I learnt from the conversation:

- Bangalore once had 1,000 lakes.
- In the 16th century, the founder of the city, Kempe Gowda, had many lakes built, so that rainwater could be stored and used for irrigation, drinking, fishing, and so on. Now, in 2024, there are less than 100.
- Pollution has become so bad that the water in most of these lakes is unfit for irrigation.
- The *raja kaluves*—natural or built canals that draw water from an overflowing lake to another—have mostly been blocked or built over. Or, buildings have come up on them.
- Ground water tables are in very bad shape because too many borewells have been dug.
- The good news is that experts believe we can turn around the situation, restoring many lakes and improving underground water levels. The bad news is that it requires a great deal of work to make people aware of these problems and find solutions. It certainly needs the support of all citizens.

I mean, it is difficult for the five of us in our loving family to decide on one thing to eat for dinner—can you imagine how difficult it would be for an entire city to come together and decide on the best way to take care of its water resources?

The anchor seemed to be having a hard time getting the guests to stop the scream fest. Amma added to the din from outside the TV.

'They should have consulted you,' said our dear Prof. Shyam Kher softly, with a smile. Appa never spoke loudly. Never wasted energy. Instead, he saved all his energy for writing scientific papers on geology and running up mountains with marathoners.

'Of course, they should have,' I said. Amma is the best in her field. I'm not saying this because I'm her daughter. There's a drawer in the study stashed with the awards she's won over the years.

Udaya High School, in all its sixty years of existence, had never seen such a shameful day. Every Foundation Day, we listened to Anandan sir talking about how his grandmother had started the school in a little by-lane in Bengaluru, and how Javaraya Avaru, a prominent horticulturist in the city, was so impressed with her dedication that he invited her to convert his bungalow into her school. Such a beautiful building. When I was little, I used to think it was huge—a grand palace.

But, over the years, I realized that it wasn't as big as Mysore Palace. Then, a couple of years back, some of the walls of the bungalow started developing cracks.

'Dear students,' Anandan sir said one day. 'As you know [why do they say it if they think we know!] our dear building needs repairs. INTACH will be taking up the restoration work. You've all heard about the Indian National Trust for Art and Cultural Heritage, haven't you? But the restoration may take at least a year to be completed.'

A collective gasp went up in the assembly. What were we going to do for a year?

'But don't worry, we will be moving temporarily to Manhattan Towers, the smart building we all know so well.'

A collective gasp went up again. No, two different sounds. One of wonder that sounded like a 'Wowww!' and the other of disbelief, like a 'Waaaat!' That glass building that was in the news for a lift disaster? No, I wanted to shout out loud. But instead, I just stood there with my mouth open. How could our small and cozy school feel at home in this garden-less, glass-encased building?

Nevertheless, we moved to Manhattan Towers in January. Why anyone would name an ugly building in the heart of Bengaluru after a city in the US I don't know. I call it MT—short for 'empty'. Empty of charm and resources. No trees around. If you look out of the window of my 6B classroom on the third floor, all you can see through the smoked glass windows are the unkempt terraces of other shorter buildings. You can also see water tanks in black and yellow, and yes, patches of solar panels.

Within a month, the school had no water, and tankers started supplying not-so-clean water. So, our make-shift playground—an unoccupied, disputed piece of land—became a messy pool of spilled water. Once in March, during our final exams, a tanker driver got into a fight with our bus driver. Oh, did I forget to mention, that because of the chaotic conditions around MT, we even had to stop using our cycles to commute to school, and that a bus had been arranged for us? Yes, so, the drivers got into a fight. That meant we were all late for the exam, and Kabir sir decided to give us all an A in history, instead of letting us write the exam. It was the only cool thing that happened during those weeks.

Summer vacation was a good break. And then when school reopened in June, so did the heavens. Rain came down in buckets, and everyone talked about how it was great for the farmers. For us though it was horrible. You know those poems about rain, and all those cute pitter-patter stories about children playing in the rain? Try getting poets and writers to wade through slushy, stinky, slippery, water-logged ground. We had to wade through the slush to reach our classrooms and be very careful not to get sucked into the open basement! But life went on, you know. Classwork, homework, silly class fights, and unit tests.

And now, even that stupid school was being shut down.

'I am Javarayyyaaa, your friendly neighbourhood ghosttt,' drawled Nakul. 'How I misssss you, my childrennn, come baaack to my schooolll!'

'Not even a ghost would want to live in a building that is falling apart,' I snapped at my silly cousin. Nakul is fifteen and has been part of a theatre club for the past three years. Looking at him now, you wouldn't know that he was once an introvert. Truth is, he had gone all quiet when his mother, my Aunt Vimla, passed away in a road accident five years ago. Then, Nakul came to stay with us. I love him and couldn't have asked for a better elder brother, but there are times when I'd happily trade him for a noisy parakeet.

The TV was on, and Sarang had changed channels. He was watching a silly cartoon. As always. Amma switched it off and walked over to the wall calendar. We must have the world's largest calendar. 'Right, so let's move on. September 25th to 28th, I'll be out. So, Shyam, you'll be in charge of the kids.

'Wait, I'll be in Namik Valley,' said Appa. 'We're taking a group of students from Visvesvaraya Uni for a run in the Himalayas.'

'Ha, mister, that's a month later,' said Amma, tapping on October with her pencil.

'Er … nope, this month. Didn't I tell you? September 22nd to 27th.'

'I'll go with Appa, you two go with Amma!' piped up Sarang.

'No way! C'mon, folks, you're old enough to stay on your own,' said Appa.

Amma considered this for a few moments. Then she declared, 'You three can come with me. With no school for goodness knows how long, you'd probably learn something at one the largest open-air museums in the world.'

'Oh, you're going back to Hampi?' said Appa. 'Awesome place, right kids? You'll love being back there. Just make sure you don't go sleuthing again like you did in Patan last year, ok?'

Patan, in Gujarat. How beautiful was Rani Ki Vav. And how lucky we were that we had found Sarang almost an anguishing hour after we realized he was missing from the world-famous stepwell.

'Come on Appa, we *had* to find Sarang, didn't we?' I defended ourselves. Appa tousled my hair and moved to the glass-shuttered wall cabinet that held his precious collection.

'I have a beautiful rock from Hampi … somewhere here … a sample that a dear colleague had given me. How I miss Pichu. It was right here…,' Appa's voice trailed off.

CORRESPONDENT
CORPORATOR
DR. RAVICHANDER

Wham! I felt like a rock had just hit me on the head! Appa's rock! I knew where it was. Not here at home. Oh no, stupid me! I don't know what had possessed me last week when I took the little rock to show to my friends in school. And I don't know what possessed me as I turned to Appa and said in my best good-girl voice, 'Appa, which kind of rock is most common in Hampi? Laterite?'

'No, no, no. You see, Hampi is part of the Dharwar craton, which is one of the oldest natural formations in India, 3.6 to 2.5 billion years old. So, the rocks you see there are....' Appa dove right into a lecture. He could be quite interesting at times, but now was *not* one of those times.

Sarang and Nakul looked at me sharply. They knew that I was side-tracking Appa. I seem to do this when I know I am in deep trouble.

Pulling me into their room, Nakul whispered, 'What have you done now?'

'That rock ... I took it to school to show it to my friends. I left it in my desk, I think. And now the school is closed. It had the prettiest natural D on it. D for Devyani—'

‘D for Dunce,’ hissed Sarang.

‘Hey, imagine what would happen if the rock and the school get buried and an archeologist found it a thousand years later and came up with an improbable theory, like … like….’

‘No, that won’t happen if you listen to me, Yan! I know how we can sneak in and bring it back without Appa ever knowing that you flicked a rock from his collection.’

‘No,’ Nakul and I barked together. Sarang’s plans were always disastrous. It is why our plan in Patan last year went wrong. But that story is for another time. Sarang’s sudden interest in detective stories in the last couple of years and his enthusiasm to rope us in had earned us the name ‘The Seekers’. I never-ever-ever want to be a seeker of *that* kind again!

The Missing Rock

As Appa prepared for his expedition to Namik Valley and Amma for her Hampi trip, we were left alone to plot and plan. After a couple of days in limbo, we got news that we would start half-day online classes soon, like we used to, during the pandemic in 2020. Meanwhile, I wondered whether I could somehow try to go to school and retrieve the rock. 'How difficult can it be? I'll just be honest and tell the guards that I left something in my desk. I'll run in and get it back,' I said in earnest.

'Ha! As if they'll let you go in!' scoffed Nakul.

'School is sealed! Didn't you see it on TV? The main entrance door is closed with a notice stuck on it,' Sarang informed me with an air of importance.

Then, he added with a cheeky smile, 'But I know how to get it.'

Desperate to get back the stone, I asked him grudgingly how we could do it.

'Simple,' he said. 'We go to Shakti Mansion, the building next to our school. Go to its terrace. Hop across to our terrace. Rappel down to the third floor of our school. Get into your classroom through the rattling window that never shuts and get the stone. Easy-peasy!'

'Nutcase! You aren't Dad. You can't rappel!'

'Don't worry, my child,' drawled Nakul, in his fake grown-up voice. 'Sri Shyam will forget all about the stone, and even if he doesn't, he will forgive you. All will be forgotten in time. Thou shalt be free of misery!'

I was aiming a pillow at him when we heard Appa's voice. 'Pichu gave me the Archean rock in June 2012 after he wound up his tenure as chief at the Anegundi site. I'd told him we'd named our baby Devyani. Hope you didn't use it as a paperweight….' I could almost visualize Amma glaring at him. She likes the old-world charm of working with paper and pencil, which meant she needed paperweights all the time.

'Hmmm…,' drawled Nakul, 'So, Sri Shyam never forgets. But we can! What do we need to pack for Hampi? You think I should take my elephant costume?'

'Sure! And maybe you can give us a ride through rocky Hampi too, Jumbo,' I said. I wasn't looking forward to this trip. Amma would be all 'wow-wow-wow-look-at-thaaat' even though she's been going to Hampi constantly for over a year now for her project. She even got me a book on the history of the Vijayanagara empire—which I've still not started reading. We had been there once before and most of the time we were with Appa, trekking. This time, with Appa out of the picture, we would have history, history, and more history. Sarang would want to keep climbing rocks like a langur. And, of course, Amma won't let him. It would be so good to just stay back in the guest house, read books, and play with the two Indies there. But that wasn't going to happen. So, I looked through my stuff and packed a few pants, tees, and other essentials.

***

It was a windy September evening when we took the metro to the railway station. Within minutes it was time to deboard. 'Nadaprabhu Kempe Gowda

Metro Station. Doors will open on the right,' said the announcer's voice.

'D'you know, Kempe Gowda was actually a chieftain of a Vijayanagara va—,' my mother began in her information service.

'—he wasn't from Bengaluru?' Sarang butted in.

'He was very much from Bengaluru, born reportedly in Yelahanka, but he was a vassal, a governor under the Vijayanagara empire. But now, let's just walk fast.'

Hmmm. 9 p.m. on a crowded elevator in Bengaluru's Krantivira Sangolli Rayanna railway station wasn't the best time to muse over historical matters. But it felt good to know that what was considered the second-largest city in the world in the 1500s had something to do with my city. Cool or what?

We boarded the Hampi Express at 10 p.m. The aisle seat that I had wrangled was totally useless since I could hardly see anything through the window. I settled down and opened the Vijayanagara book. The train's light showed patches of fields now and then. It was pitch dark beyond. How do people live in such places, I wondered. Aren't they afraid of creepy things crawling over them? My train of thought took me to other people who lived in the wild. Well, places without street lights. As the train swayed rhythmically, the book I was trying to read slipped down from my hands, my eyes seemed to close, my mind relaxed, and I wondered how Hakka and Bukka would have felt while riding their horses.

Danger in Anegundi

1335, Anegundi

The Tungabhadra flowed boldly through the rocks.

'Let's jump into the river!' Guna said as he dismounted from his old horse.

'And get swept off?' mocked his elder brother, Viju. 'We can take a dip further down the river.' The boys had ridden ahead of their elders, who were riding reverentially behind Hakka Raya and Bukka Raya, the heroic Sangama brothers who had fought for King Kampili Deva.

'How long do you think they will take to catch up with us?' asked Guna, cheekily. He prided himself on being the fastest youngster on a horse.

'Hmm. I'm sure they have stopped at the *thenginkayi toppu* now,' Viju said, referring to the coconut grove en route. 'Appa must be climbing up a tree to get the best coconuts for our princes.'

Hakka and Bukka were not really of royal lineage. Sons of Bhavana Sangama, they once lived in Warangal and fought in the war there but were forced to flee to a small kingdom called Kampili. When Muhammad bin Tughluq's army from the Sultanate of Delhi invaded Kampili, the Sangama brothers fought hard, but they had to leave that kingdom too. The only Hindu kingdom in the region that was left unconquered was Hoysala. Now, the brothers were very keen to win back the territories that their late king had lost. But many of their friends had died during the battles. They had to get away from Hoysala to create and train a whole new army of soldiers. Guna and Viju would have preferred not to be soldiers. But what else could they be when their father and uncles were all in the new army?

Now, the boys strolled ahead, after tying their horses to a tree. Jumping over boulders and sliding down some of the bigger ones, Viju came to what looked like a cave. He ran in. 'Guna, come here! Quick!'

What he saw stunned Guna. 'Who could have done this?' he exclaimed, looking at the brick-coloured paintings on the walls. 'Rajaratnam *thathagaru*?'

'No! Why would the most celebrated artist of the Hoysala kingdom paint in a cave in the middle of nowhere? Anyway, he is now in Delhi, and his characters have many more details. These are crudely drawn, but look, is that a tiger? Or leopard?'

The boys ran their hands over the walls. 'I think this must be a hundred years old,' said Viju.

'Thousand,' countered Guna.

'Many thousands maybe. The paintings have stayed hidden here, away from sunlight and rain all this time. I wonder what they used to make this red pigment. Ugh, but what a stink. Come, come, let's go tell Hakka raja about this place.... Oh, by the way, I heard that he is looking for a suitable spot to set up a new kingdom,' Viju added in a whisper. But Guna was nowhere to be seen. Excited, he had sauntered on, going deeper into the dark depths of the cave.

'Guna? Guna, where are you? GUNA!'

Viju's voice echoed inside the cave.

The figures on the walls were all holding hands and seemed to be dancing. And here was his kid brother, not even wanting to stick close to him. 'Guna!'

Maybe Guna was already with the horses, Viju thought. But he was not there either. The horses seemed restless. And Viju saw something on the ground that made him freeze in fright. Fresh leopard scats.

'Shhh … I'm up here,' whispered Guna from the top of a huge boulder. 'The smell in the cave did make me wonder if we were inside a leopard's cave. I did not want to scare you. So, I came out just in time to chase a weary leopard away from his own home. Poor chap. He went that way. C'mon, let's get out of here before he returns.'

Guna slid down the rock, mounted the horse, and waited for his brother to mount his horse. As they rode closer to the riverbank, they saw the party ahead, trying to cross the river at its narrowest. The dogs and horses seemed to love the water. When the team came up on the other side of the river, Hakka and Bukka raced ahead. The others followed. Once on higher ground, the dogs were chasing some startled rabbits.

'Rabbit for lunch today?' said Hakka. He looked around in awe. 'Bukka, do you see what I see?'

Bukka too was looking ahead, awestruck. A saint was sitting under the shadow of a rock. He bowed his head and fell at the saint's feet.

'Rise and shine,' said the sage. 'Isn't this a lovely place? I think there is something special about this place … it makes everyone brave,' he said gently.

Hakka and Bukka looked at each other. Then Hakka said, 'This is where we should build our new kingdom. The river below would be a natural moat. We'll build a fortress here.'

Guna felt sorry for the rabbits that would soon end up in a pot or be chased away from the site of the new kingdom. Meanwhile, Viju looked around at the huge boulders. How could anything be built on this dry, arid land, he wondered. In his young mind, a picture arose of a large body of water right in the middle of a busy kingdom. Of a city where people could live without fear of invading armies and spend their days growing fruits and vegetables in well-watered fields.

Guna too imagined a beautiful kingdom. Of a place so harmonious that even invaders would change their

minds and become their partners in trade. He had heard about travellers from faraway places coming to a port near Thoothukudi to trade in pearls and spices, hundreds of years ago. He had heard of the Cholas travelling across the seas to carry out trade with other countries. Why fight when one could live and let live, he thought. Young Viju and Guna savoured their daydreams of peace and prosperity.

History would record that period as the birth of Vijayanagara. Historians argued hundreds of years later that the credit for establishing the Vijayanagara empire should actually go to the Hoysala king Veera Ballala III, who named it after his son Beeja—as Beejanuggur—and that Ballala III appointed his very capable chieftain Hakka as *mahamandalesvara*—or chief—of the new city. Some others argue that Hampi had for long been associated with different dynasties—Kadamba, Chalukya of Badami, Hoysala, Kalachuri, and Yadava. That Muhammed Bin Tughlaq captured the Sangama brothers, and later sent them back as governors of the region and that the brothers broke free, and set up the kingdom of Vijayanagara. Legend would add that the name and the place were actually suggested by a saint called Vidyaranya. Viju had heard his father saying that the saint came here all the way from Sringeri on the other side of the great Sahyadri mountains.

And here they were—Vijendra and Gunasekara—from Anegundi, just across the Pampa river, named after the Goddess Pampa. An ancient but small Shiva shrine seemed to welcome them to this new land. Who knew then that Viju and Guna were on the verge of helping the Sangama brothers establish a great city that would be called Hampi, with its famous Virupaksa temple.

Off to Hampi

'Get up, Dee!' said Nakul, tugging on my blanket. 'Have we already reached Hospete?' I asked, loathe to get out of the gently rocking train. I groaned, remembering parts of my dream. Or, was it the story I was reading that involved two boys on horses and the younger one fighting an angry leopard? Wait! Was that Sarang? I looked around wildly and saw an angelic Sarang walking behind Amma, as they made their way towards the door. I gulped some water from my flask, then picked up my knapsack, and stumbled along behind them. 'Sarang, did you see a leopard last night?' I asked my brother.

'What? Where, here?' he asked in a panic. Ha, what a relief! That was a dream after all.

'C'mon, c'mon, get down first, talk later,' said Amma. 'And stop teasing the baby, Yan,' she continued, using the short name I liked. For some reason, I do not like it when people call me Devi.

We tumbled into the SUV that the guest house had sent to pick up Amma. As far as the eye could see there were hillocks of giant boulders. How had the boulders stayed put for millions of years? They looked like they could roll down and crash into us any minute. In the plains between the hills were fields of paddy, banana, and coconut. The drive had been quite pleasant, which made it all the more jarring when the car turned into a compound with a low, old building. We'd reached the guest house.

The sun was almost up by now, and I wondered what was in store for us. Maybe, just maybe, I'd be lucky to find a small stone with a D on it, similar to Appa's stone. I mean, it was possible, right? Miracles do happen, don't they?

'Kids, get ready quick,' said Amma, pushing me through a long corridor. 'Boys, your room is upstairs. Come down in time for breakfast at eight, ok? I have to be at the site by nine.'

I followed Amma and the usher to a room with tiles so bright that my morning eyes felt achy. I like colourful things, but this was a bit too gaudy. I wish we could have stayed at one of the houses that Amma keeps talking about. The ones in Anegundi across the river. It seems many houses there have been re-constructed in the old style but with modern amenities. Old doors, windows, and frames had been removed from the crumbling buildings and re-used in the new ones.

The boys ran up to their room. Shortly after, we assembled at the dining area. The steaming hot idlis and vada were just what I needed though Sarang made a fuss. As usual. Nakul asked for extra cups of sambar. 'We'll be in a car soon and driving through rough roads,' warned Amma.

Soon, we got into an SUV and proceeded to the temporary office of Ambara Constructions. Amma had informed us that the company was planning to develop a huge tourism project on both banks of the main branch of the river. They had done a feasibility study as was required. Amma's role, among many other things, was to see if the study had been conducted correctly, and if construction could be permitted.

The minute we entered the office, two or three people rushed to greet Amma and smiled kindly at us. Too kindly! Again, I wished I could have stayed back at the guest house. Amma introduced us and then promptly informed them that we would be happy to stay in the library since we were all book lovers. Sarang looked up sharply, and his eyes seemed to shout, 'Amma, you liar!' Thankfully, the officers

did not see that look. The 'library' was nothing more than a large room with a central table that had about twenty different journals displayed on top, and a few books kept in a small glass cupboard. It looked like Dr Inamdar's dental clinic—ouch! Nakul was soon lost in his mobile phone. Sarang walked from one window to another. 'Yan, look, monkeys! On top of our car.'

I put back the magazine I'd picked up and went to the window. The *langurs* looked at us as though *we* were monkeys. One of them was looking at something in his hands. 'That's a phone. Monkey with a phone!' Sarang shouted. 'And look, the driver's window is open.'

Our driver must have heard Sarang because he came running to shoo away the animals. 'Anna, Anna, phone,' Sarang shouted.

'Huh? Oh, not mine,' he said, not bothering to go after the monkey with the phone.

'We have to do something! Nakul, Yan, come! Let's try to retrieve the phone.'

Hearing the commotion, a man came out of the conference room and asked us if we wanted anything.

'No, no, but look, that monkey has taken away somebody's phone, and it's sitting right there. Shouldn't we go after it?'

'Oh that. Can't do anything about it. Monkeys are always stealing something or the other here,' he said. 'They like phones very much. That's why we don't carry expensive phones in this area. Will the owner get back the phone? Who knows,' he said, spreading his palms and looking up at the sky as though to say only divine powers could now decide the phone's fate.

After what seemed like a million hours, Amma and a few people emerged from the room. We were to go to Anegundi on the other side of the river.

'I'll keep you posted, Bhupati sir,' said Amma. She spoke firmly.

Bhupati gave her a wide smile. 'Madam, we know you will like our plan. We know you will make a very fair and detailed analysis of our new scheme, Madam. You know how important it is for us, right? It is in the best interest of *namma Hampe*! Dear Hampi! We'll be waiting to hear from you, Madam.

'Oh, by the way, there has been an accident on the bridge, Madam. Traffic pile-up. Just like in your Bengaluru,' Bhupati said, with an almost too eager smile. 'That is why you'll have to get down from the car at the riverbank and go in a coracle across the river, Madam.'

How nice! I would love to go on a coracle—the small, round boat with a wooden frame used in this region.

Then he turned to the man who had come out earlier to talk to us. 'Krishna, take Madam and her family to the Anegundi site. Drive very carefully, ok? And make sure they are all secure in the coracle, ok? Be careful when you cross the river too. Bye, children, don't dip your hands in the river. It may look calm and harmless but there may be crocodiles lurking around. Enjoy the trip to the site. See you soon, Madam.'

Was it possible for someone to look anxious, over-polite, and menacing, all at once? I seemed to recognize a hint of all this in Bhupati sir's silky voice.

Nakul was reading something on his phone. Then he tapped Amma and whispered, 'Brimma, look, there's no accident or pile-up on the bridge. Traffic is quite smooth.' Brimma was what Nakul called his Brinda *dodamma*.

'Huh? Maybe it happened just now?' she said.

'No! This is a police traffic app that shows live location and information.'

'But Nakul, why do you have this app? Just because your parents....'

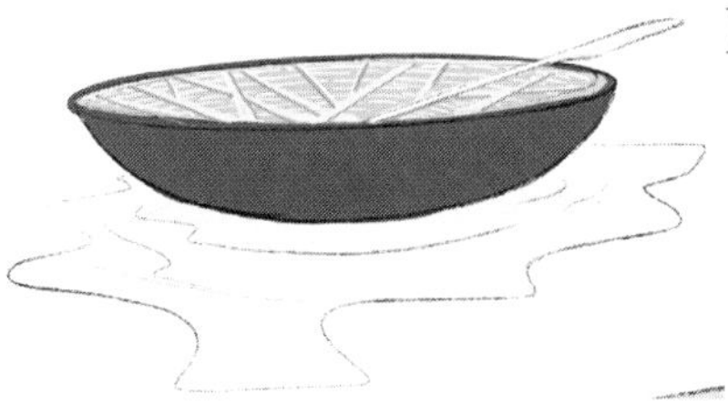

I wasn't listening to Amma anymore. I could only hear Bhupati sir's voice in my head. A chill ran down my spine. What had Amma got into? Was there a threat hanging over her? Or was I just imagining it?

The Bukka Aqueduct

Just as we trooped into the car, there was a call from Appa. Amma spoke for a bit and then put the phone on speaker. 'Hi folks, how's it going? Off to Anegundi?' Appa's voice came through.

'Appa, Devyani is trembling. She thinks we're going to be pushed into the river,' piped up Sarang.

'What? Why? Brinda, what's happening?'

Amma looked stunned too and turned to Sarang. He looked guilty because I'd sworn him to secrecy. 'Yan says the man who was in Amma's meeting is scary and was threatening her,' he said in a rush.

Amma snatched the phone. 'No problem, Shyam, everything is fine here. You allow these kids to watch too many crime serials with you.'

'With me? I can't watch those serials on my own … they give me nightmares! Ok, ok, forget I said that,' mumbled Appa. 'Kids, be careful. None of your stunts, do you hear me? And take care of each other. And, guess what? We're at Namik village, and I had the most amazing dish made with freshly harvested rajma. This place is charming … so many sulphur springs and waterfalls. That's how the place gets its name Namik, from *namak* … salt. It's so cool that you're going to cross a river, and we're going to try to cross a river too—the Ramganga, which is fed by the Namik glacier. Miss you folks. Take care.'

We knew Appa was trying to be brave. I mean, why else would he try to sound cool by using words like 'it's so cool', which he normally never did.

'Don't worry, Appa,' I said. 'Even if they push Amma out of the coracle, we'll do fine. We're a super swimmer family, remember? And anyway, Sarang hasn't had a bath in ages—'

'—just saving water,' butted in Sarang, punching me on the arm.

Amma gave me a sudden hug. 'We'll be fine, Yan, don't worry.'

I had many questions for her, but by then Krishnanna—we added an 'anna' out of respect to all the male adults we ever met—had got into the car. If he was Bhupati's colleague, maybe he was his friend too. And I did not want to talk about my fears in front of him.

After a ten-minute drive through Hampi, we reached the riverbank. Several coracles were waiting to ferry people across the river. The one we got into was large enough to accommodate all six of us. I'd read somewhere that in the olden days, even horses and goats would be transported on coracles. The gentle movement of the boat and the calm breeze lulled us into a gentle reverie. Even Sarang stopped chattering. Nakul was taking pictures on his phone. And Amma kept making notes as she spoke to Krishnanna.

On the other side of the river, a van waited for us. 'Welcome, welcome Brinda madam! Your children? My name is Mahayuta, but you can call me Mahi!'

Amma waved at him and made some pleasant comments, and then we were off again.

'I'll take you to Bukka's aqueduct first,' said Mahi. He turned to us and started firing questions. 'You know what an aqueduct is, right? It is how people in the highlands got water from the river in this valley. Fascinating, no?'

At a distance, we saw something that looked like the ruins of a Roman structure that I had once seen on TV. Made of huge blocks of rock, it looked like a bridge.

'I could make such a cool reel if we could only get on that bridge,' Nakul said wistfully.

'But why is the bridge so narrow?' Sarang said. 'Not enough space even for a motorbike to go on it.'

'It isn't a bridge, it's an aqueduct. To transport water.'

'Then why is it over the river?' asked Sarang.

'Wait, wait, I'll explain everything. What a treat is waiting for you,' said Mahi. 'Isn't it just beautiful? Our citizen's group has just petitioned the government to renovate it. Your mother is going to—'

'Shh Mahi,' admonished Amma. 'No discussing projects with outsiders, remember?'

'Your *own* children are outsiders?' I said, hurt.

Amma just gave me a look.

'Right, let me then tell you just about this ancient aqueduct of the Vijayanagara empire,' said Mahi. 'The empire flourished only because its leaders gave a lot of importance to water management. They wanted water for their own lavish baths too. Swimming pools, even! And, of course, for their gardens. But what was most important to them was irrigation. Better irrigation meant better crops, and better crops meant better income for the rulers. You see, instead of paying income tax in money like we do now, the dynasty required all farmers to give a percentage of their produce as tax. So, the rulers invested heavily in building water tanks, canals, and aqueducts to bring water from lakes and rainwater pits to the city of Hampi.'

Mahi stopped the car by the side of the road, and we got down and walked to the aqueduct. How did they stack such enormous blocks of stone?

'The kings loved to flaunt their priceless jewels, but they were even prouder to show off the agricultural prosperity of their region. No person who came seeking assistance to improve irrigation was turned away without a handsome loan. Paddy, fruit, cane, and coconut plantations grew lush and bountiful. If a minister suggested that a new canal be made, the kings were always ready. The flow of water was smooth, constant, and generous for all citizens.'

'Did the rulers control the farmers?' said Nakul.

'No, not at all. Researchers claim that while the rulers wanted some control over irrigation, they were happy for others to take on the responsibility of running irrigation-related activities on their own. People were able to follow their own local traditions and customs as far as agriculture was concerned. In short, a live and let live policy.'

As Mahi continued to speak, the car rattled on, and the endless piles of rocks sat silently in the sun. My mind drifted away to another place and another time.

Viju's Talented Granddaughter

1407, Vijayanagara

Viju looked at his granddaughter, Shubha, making a complex design on the floor. It certainly did not look like the rangoli she was supposed to be making. 'What is that, young lady?' he said.

'Look Thathagaru, this is a lake on the eastern flank of Saptagiri. Is there a way to get that water to our city? Water always flows to a lower level, right? So, can't we cut a gorge in the hills to bring that water here?'

Viju often recalled the day in the caves when he and his brother Guna could have been mauled by a leopard. The boys knew that these big cats preferred to avoid humans than attack them. But what if it had attacked them in self-defence? The brothers got

lucky that day. Not just that, they had survived many wars. He felt proud that they had achieved many feats together. Guna had become a most trusted emissary and often travelled to different kingdoms to build trade relations. Viju, meanwhile, had enjoyed helping Hakka and Bukka of the Sangama dynasty build a new city, slowly and quietly, so as not to be noticed by invaders.

When Veera Bukka Raya ascended the throne, people likened the new capital of Vijayanagara to a radiant jewel nestled in the heart of the Tungabhadra river, which flowed round it like a pearl necklace.

It took many years to transform Vijayanagara into the 'supreme city' that it came to be known as. How busy and how exciting those years were. The empire had grown so much that they now controlled the doab—a tract of land lying between two converging rivers. In this case, it lay between the Krishna and Tungabhadra rivers. Of course, they controlled other regions too, like Goa in the west and Jaffna and Malabar in the south.

Hakka's son, Harihara Raya II, had continued the good work of his uncle Bukka. How busy those years with him were—so much had happened in twenty-seven years. And then there was the bad phase. Viju remembered how disturbed he was when Harihara II died, and how much he had tried to mediate and drill some sense into the three sons of Harihara II. But no, they fought and fought and fought. One of the three, Virupaksa Raya, was murdered by his own sons. Viju shuddered as he thought about the many times Vijayanagara had been attacked from within and by other kingdoms.

'Thathagaru, where have you gone?' asked Shubha.

Viju forced his mind back to the present. The past was in the past. It was 1407 now. Deva Raya I was ruling Vijayanagara. Construction of dams and canals had continued over the years. As people from far and near visited the kingdom and thousands came to work and stay on at Vijayanagara, the need for water continued in the ever-growing city. What more could be done? Viju enjoyed coming up with solutions even though he was now in his eighties.

Yet, nothing could top the joy Viju felt watching his sixteen-year-old granddaughter coming up with brilliant ideas. Shubha seemed to have inherited his love for dreaming up solutions. 'Hmmm, an idea worth considering, Shubha. What do you think would happen if the water flowed for a long distance in this hot weather?'

'Oh, some of it would seep into the hills. Some would evaporate. So, my idea isn't so great after all, is it?' mumbled Shubha and proceeded to tear up the drawing she had made.

'Stop! Now let's see if we can prevent a bit of seepage and a bit of evaporation. How can we do that?'

'Could we lay stone slabs in a row so that most of the water would flow over the stones instead of seeping into the ground?' Shubha wondered aloud.

'Excellent idea!'

'Thathagaru! I know that voice. It means you've already done this, right? You're just humouring me.'

'You're sixteen, Rani, I am eighty-eight. I don't think I came up with ideas like this when I was your age.'

'Thathagaru, can you please show me your drawings of the city you had imagined? Can I take them out?'

Viju smiled at his granddaughter. Together, they opened a large, wooden trunk. It contained many rolls of parchment scrolls and many writings on palm leaves.

'So beautiful, Thathagaru.'

'The paper? Your *chinnthathagaru*, Guna, was given a role of it as a gift from a trader who had brought it all the way from Kashmir. And Guna gave it to me. Wait, I think I have a small unused piece left … here, would you like to have it?'

'The paper is lovely. But I meant your writing. How I wish I could draw and paint like you.'

One of the things that excited Viju the most was the aqueduct they were presently designing, which would carry water from Anegundi, across the Tungabhadra, to the vast city of Hampi. Deva Raya I had personally taken an interest in the project and come up with some brilliant suggestions. He was a ruler who strongly believed that water sources and their management were crucial for a kingdom—for a happy, healthy, and prosperous kingdom!

Pointing to the drawing of a small structure across a part of the Tungabhadra, he explained, 'Look, this is where we got the rocks from. Many workers worked for long hours, coaxing trained elephants to move the rocks to the river bed. Then, we built a cleverly shaped structure called an anicut. This anicut was built on the river, so that the flow could be regulated and some of the water could be stored for later use. We had to align the boulders in such a way that they would reduce the speed of the water but still allow it to pass. Otherwise, the banks could get flooded during the rains. The angle of the anicut had to be calculated in such a way that a part of the water could be diverted to different directions and into different canals, but much of the silt wasn't carried forward. Otherwise, the silt would block the canals.'

'And how did you know where to build these structures? Where to build the temples and palaces?' Shubha asked.

'Observation! Listening to nature. When you observe nature, you realize that some places are fertile, some are marshy, and some are hard and unyielding. You can see trees growing tall and strong in some places on their own. So, it was common sense to use the most fertile areas for irrigation. We planned to build and expand the city only on the most useless land.'

'But how could you survive on an arid land? Didn't you need water to drink and for your other needs?'

'Ah, so that's the reason we started looking at places in the hills where rainwater tends to collect. We created trenches and percolation pits on these hillsides, allowing some of the rainwater to seep into the ground and saturate it. The rest of the water was made to flow towards water bodies like a *pushkarini*. Settlements could come up around such waterbodies.'

'So, you used many methods to bring water to different parts of the city.'

'Yes, and now we're working to build a dam across the river. It's one of Deva Raya's most ambitious plans. I don't know if I'll still be around when it is completed.'

'Thathagaru, don't say things like that! Of course, you'll live for a long, long time.'

Viju just laughed and helped Shubha put back the scrolls. It was unbelievable how the kingdom had continued to grow despite the wars against neighbouring kingdoms. Trade continued as well. In fact, Guna had helped the king get horses from as far as Arabia and Persia.

The Dramatic Mr Chandru

The car stopped.

'You dozed off again?' said Amma. 'Didn't you see the canals on the way?'

'Oh … umm … of course I saw them,' I said. I wasn't lying. I had seen the canals in my dream—in Viju's drawings—right?

'Want to see my pictures of the canals? I have tonnes,' Nakul said, shoving his phone into my face.

'No, Ma, she was sleeping. Snoring in fact!'

I made a face at Sarang.

'Ok, tell me how many monkeys were sitting on that little temple we crossed?'

'Five,' I said, taking a wild guess.

'Ha! Fifteen! So, now tell the truth, were you sleeping, or can you not count?'

'Mahi sir, how long is this aqueduct? Looks so fascinating,' I said, faking great interest.

'Whoa, Dee-Dee's diversion tactics,' Nakul exclaimed.

Mahi sir took off on another lecture, sounding very much like dear Appa on one of his geology wonders. Suddenly I felt uneasy. Appa's rock—that lovely D-rock. What would Appa say when he learnt what I had done with it? How could I have been so silly?

***

After a long day, and the best *thindi* of *avalakki vade* at a small café in Anegundi, we crossed the river (no one got pushed into the water). But I could not shake off that dull ache in my heart.

Amma too seemed to have a lot on her mind. When we were having dinner at the guest house, she broke one of the family's cardinal rules and continued to look into her phone where she had made her notes. She did not notice my face. Nakul did. 'What's come over you now? Why that face?' Who knew brothers could be so perceptive?

'Nothing,' I said nonchalantly.

'She's missing Growly ma'am's history classes,' said Sarang, in a sing-song voice.

'Stop it, I'm not missing anything or anybody.' But he must have caught the break in my voice for he said softly, as though I were his kid sister, 'Missing Appa? Or his stone, huh? I told you I can get it for you.'

I concentrated on my food. No one in the long, long history of Hampi could have ever shown more interest in cabbage *palya* than I did then at that moment. Back in the room, Amma whipped out her laptop, possibly transferring her notes, videos, and voice notes from her phone.

'It's an important day tomorrow. Very important,' she said. She was frowning as her eyes darted from her phone to her laptop. I drifted off to sleep.

The next morning, as we gathered at the dining room, Amma was all bright and cheerful. 'We'll be visiting the pushkarini near the Vittala temple. You remember the stepwell, right? You know, some years ago, they were trying to restore this tank. They decided to remove the water fully, desilt it, and then put it back. But it just wouldn't empty! An architect came to do a study and helped the Archaeological Society of India discover the most interesting water management system—hundreds of years old. And it still works! Amazing, isn't it?'

'Desilt is to remove mud and sand from the bottom of a river or pond, right?' Sarang said.

I was surprised at his genuine question. I mean, it was Sarang asking a legitimate question! 'Yes,' I added quickly. 'It is so the water stays clean and flows better.'

Didn't I tell you that my mom loves everything about Hampi and its 'brilliant use of natural resources'. But, I agreed—it was incredible that a system set up by the Vijayanagara kings was still in working order today.

'Anyway, you three can come to the pushkarini too, and after that I've asked Chandru to take you around the complex. I'll be heading back to the project office. I'll join you around five, ok?'

'What, a tour of Hampi again?' groaned Sarang.

'Oh, I love Chandranna's style, he's so dramatic,' said Nakul. The last time we were here, he had told us many things about Vijayanagara. Somehow, one piece of information stayed in my mind, and I can clearly recall him saying this: This capital of Vijayanagara is blessed because, even though the rainfall here is not much and somewhat unpredictable, it is built near a sort of large alluvial bowl created by the broad bend of our dear Tungabhadra.

❋❋❋

Mr Chandru—as most people called him, but he was Chandranna to us kids—was, indeed, a very lively person. And, he had the sweetest companion. A brown Indie called Kaapi. There were about a dozen tourists in his group including us. Kaapi sniffed everyone discreetly, then stayed by Chandranna's side. The weather was perfect for a walk around Hampi's ancient temples. A good night's sleep must have helped, for I felt more energetic and cheerful.

The pushkarini was beautiful. Set against the boulders beyond, the large man-made tank collected rainwater. Water also filtered into it through a series

of small ponds dug across the hills. The run-off water would magically percolate down to this well, said our guide. I felt like running down the steps and touching the water. It looked as though white bales of cotton were floating in the water, but, of course, these were reflections of the sky. While Amma and her colleagues continued with their discussion, the boys and I carefully went down the ancient stone steps towards the water. 'Never dries up even during the summer, it seems,' observed Nakul.

I glanced up the steps to see Amma pointing to the hills and tapping on her phone emphatically. Her curly hair flew wildly in the strong wind. Her colleagues seemed equally animated. That—*that* man had joined them too now. A chill ran down my spine when I noticed how he kept looking at Amma and all that she was jotting down. He seemed polite enough but I just did not have a good feeling about him. Trying not to think unpleasant thoughts, I concentrated on following the boys down the stepwell.

'Appa would have loved this! Look at these stones. Wow!' said Sarang.

'The pushkarini must be full in the rainy season, right? Wonder if we can swim to that small pavilion in the centre … would be so awesome,' remarked Nakul.

The mention of rains made my mind jump to thoughts about the heavy rains reported in Bengaluru. Thoughts about our school. About it getting submerged? Would my rock get displaced from the desk? Where was it now? Rolling on the floor somewhere? Blocking the little outlet for water in our classroom?

Stop it, silly, I told myself with a sudden shrug. Our classroom was on the third floor. And our city only got a few millimetres of rain each time. It wasn't going to be swept off in a tsunami! And, yet, I had that dull, achy feeling. After all, rain *did* get into our classroom. The windows were so badly made that we never could close them. What if the rain got in and—? Stop, I begged myself. These thoughts just had to go!

Amma and her colleagues left after half an hour. We stayed on at the complex, with Chandranna going nonstop with the history lessons. The sun was beating down on us hard. Thankfully, I'd picked up the most beautiful sun-hat made of banana fibre from a craft shop in Anegundi.

Shortly after, our group made its way towards the Virupaksa temple, the oldest temple in Hampi. A large number of langurs and bonnet macaques seemed to be watching the people around them with great interest.

'Hide your phones, zip your bags,' Chandranna barked out his orders before continuing with the story. 'This was once the richest bazaar in the world. Now close your eyes, wipe out the images of all these chips packets hanging in the shops, and imagine bazaars of gold and gems instead. Yes, these bazaars sold gold and silver coins and gems of different kinds from distant lands. Think of them as malls, but in the open. Vendors vied for attention, showing off their stunning wares. Kings and their ministers from faraway places often came incognito, trying to gather clues about how business was being done. Can you imagine that? The horses and elephants would be tethered there,' he said, pointing. 'That was the old parking place.'

As we walked around the temple, Chandranna told us that it had been a small shrine when the Sangama brothers first came to Hampi. 'Then, it was expanded and developed further by each ruler. Look at this trough carved out of a huge block of stone. It was to store water for animals.'

We followed like sheep behind Chandranna. The Hampi monuments are stunning but trying to see all of them at once can be pretty tiring—both mentally and physically. I wouldn't have minded taking in all this while sitting atop an elephant.

I was lost in my thoughts, tired from all the walking, when suddenly Sarang's voice cut through. He was running ahead and shouting, 'Hey, look, this looks like such a cool water slide.' Picking up a stone, he aimed to throw it into one of the interconnected, raised, long stone troughs near us.

'Stop it, you fool, I'm sure you're not supposed to do that,' said Nakul.

'But what do you think will happen if I drop a smooth rock here?'

'A guard will catch you and shout at you! Or, maybe—can you see those two pillars there?—tie you up to them and have your head cut off,' Nakul said in a menacing filmy 'villain' voice.

'The stone would roll down slowly along the troughs, and…' I trailed off, taking in the wonder of what I now knew was part of a watercourse that included an aqueduct. The stone would roll down the long slide and fall into the stepwell, just like the water that flowed in from a distant source into a tank or stepwell. This is how water was brought here from Lake Kamalapura, located a few kilometres away. How beautiful! 'Can you imagine that this water channel is maybe five hundred years old?' I mused.

'Devyani *avare*, you should stay on in Hampi and become a guide,' said Nakul. After more walking in the sun and seeing more monuments, including the stone chariot, and doing touristy things like posing against it with a fifty-rupee note featuring the monument, we finally sat down under a tree. It looked really old. It had a million wrinkles or whatever old trees have.

'This is a plumeria tree. It is called temple tree and is often found around the temples of India and Sri Lanka. Can you guess its age?' Chandranna asked.

'Forty?' ventured a young lady in our group.

'More like hundred and forty,' he replied. 'Maybe more. Some people say it might have been given as a gift by the Portuguese traveller and historian Domingo Paes in the early 1500s.'

'And how does he know how old the tree is? Just exaggeration,' whispered Nakul to me.

'Shh…,' I admonished him, intrigued by the tale of a foreigner bringing a sapling or seed and presenting it to a king.

'How do you think all our olden civilizations were so advanced? They learnt from one another. They were brave. They fought each other, yes. But they also invited learned travellers to their courts. How many of you have seen the Turthu canal? Deva Raya I got it built around 1410. That's more than 600 years ago! How did he get the idea? Was he the first to come up with ideas for water management like that? Who knows…. The Chalukyas of Badami further north had very good water management systems too. How did they know so much hundreds of years ago in 600 to 800 CE? So many questions, no?'

'Ha! I'm sure he doesn't know the answers to most of these. He doesn't have to answer questions like us in exams,' murmured Nakul.

Chandranna took a deep breath and wiped his brow, as though he had single-handedly lifted rocks to build a dam. 'Ancient inscriptions on rocks tell us many things about the past. As I said, kings fought against each other, conquered regions, and learnt from each other. Could Deva Raya have been inspired by the *anaikattu* built sometime in the year 150 to 200 that still functions today? It's on the River Cauvery. Anyone?'

'Kallanai, also called the Grand Anicut,' said an old woman in the audience. She must be a professor, I thought.

'Right, amma, brilliant,' said our guide.

'Kallanai, which literally means "stone dam" in Tamil, was built by Karikala Cholan of the Chola dynasty. An anicut is a simple form of a dam. It is built by placing huge rocks, stones, and other local natural materials across a river or part of a river. This allows some water to be stored in places, while the rest of it flows down as streams. The king fought and overpowered the Sinhalese kingdom and imprisoned thousands of soldiers. He is believed to have brought them to the Chola kingdom and got them to build the dam.'

The quizzing continued as he made us walk to another monument. Kaapi was now coming to me often. It was nearly lunchtime when we came to a strange row of stone blocks. Ah, the famous dining tables of Hampi! It is believed that the soldiers of Vijayanagara used to eat at this table.

'Here are two rows of stone dining tables, with carved-out plates and cups. A canal ran between the tables with flowing water. The men could wash their "plates" and hands right here in the flowing water. Imagine that! A channel of water, instead of the little finger bowls we get in hotels today,' Chandranna said, laughing at his own words.

I wish we could have ordered some food online like we did back home and eaten it in this quaint, historical place. But of course that was not allowed. So, off we trudged through the ruins to a pretty restaurant under mango trees and facing the Tungabhadra.

'I can't believe it,' I said, as I mused over the mounds of historical information we received that day.

'A carved, stone dining table?' said Nakul.

'No, you nutcase, I can't believe that thing about bringing people from outside his kingdom,' I retorted. 'How and why would a south Indian king go across the land, cross the Bay of Bengal, attack Sri Lanka, and bring the prisoners of war back to work for him? How? I mean, how could they even bring thousands of people across in those days?'

Yes, I'd listened very carefully to the guide for a change.

'That's what surprises you? How about the fact that hundreds of elephants were being exported from Ceylon, too?' said Nakul.

He fished out his phone and checked the location of the anicut, whether it was still there, and how far Ceylon was from Kallanai near Thanjavur. Then he looked up a map of the old Chola kingdom of south India. 'Here's the Cauvery, and here is the Tungabhadra.' We studied the map for a long time, trying to understand this part of history.

Why people would go to all this trouble was beyond me. I mean, did they really use local elephants and imported horses to move around? As for me, I just wanted to get back to the guest house and chill out. We kept looking out for Amma, who seemed to be taking forever to join us.

'What shall we do tomorrow?' Nakul said. 'Maybe we should check to see if there is a play running or something,' he added. We'd watched a thrilling *yakshagana* show the last time we were in Hampi.

Who knew then that a real-life drama awaited us later in the day?

The shadows of the *gopuras* and the ruins were growing longer. Though the monuments were beautiful, I felt my head would burst with the overdose of information. I really didn't want to stay any longer, and I was hoping Amma would return soon. Did she expect us to stick around for the light and sound show, I wondered.

Suddenly, Nakul's phone rang. 'Unknown number,' he mumbled and ignored it. It rang again. This time, he cut it after a couple of rings. It rang again. He let it ring. For a long time.

Can a phone ring sound—what's that word?—opi … oni … ominous? It did to me. Very.

Where's Amma?

Appa and Amma have drilled it into Nakul that he is not to take calls from unknown numbers or open any suspicious links received on the phone. Sarang and I did not have mobile phones of course. 'But what if it is from Appa on a borrowed phone? Remember, on his last run, he'd left his phone at the base camp,' said Sarang.

The phone kept ringing. And finally, Nakul answered it. 'What? Her phone is missing? Oh, oh ok, sir, thank you for letting us know about her plans. Yes, yes, thank you.'

'Who was that? Amma's phone is missing? Was it the monkeys? Where is Amma?' I said, my words tumbling out in a rush.

'Which question should I answer first, Devi ji?' chided my dear cousin. 'Brimma's phone is missing. They've been looking for it, and yes, they think a monkey might have slunk away with it. Or, that she may have left it unattended at one of the sites they visited. This man … her colleague it seems … said they were all still at a meeting, and that she will return late. So we need to get back to the guest house on our own.'

'Wait! That doesn't sound like Amma at all! I mean, if she lost her phone, wouldn't she be the first to quickly borrow a colleague's phone and tell us that herself?' I reasoned.

'The guy said she's in a meeting, Yan,' said Nakul, his voice high-pitched.

'Well, then how come he, her colleague, could make a call?' argued Sarang. He jumped up and grabbed Nakul's phone. 'Let's call back and ask to talk to her.'

Nakul dialled the number.

No answer.

And, then, the phone went dead.

We looked at each other, confused.

We were quiet for a few minutes. It was one of those moments when you feel a dark cloud hanging over you, with a dagger or sword—or something like that—hidden inside, waiting to fall any second.

'Let's try again,' I said quietly. 'Maybe the phone was out of charge.'

Nakul tried. Still switched off.

'Let's call Appa,' suggested Sarang.

'No, let's not worry him. What can he do from so far away?'

'Of course he'll be able to help. Appa is the greatest,' said Sarang roundly.

'Hey kids, aren't we over-reacting? I mean, Brimma must be in the midst of something important. She'll call us soon … I think,' said Nakul. It was clear from his voice that even he wasn't convinced with his argument.

Sarang yanked the mobile from Nakul's hand and called Appa.

'Speaker,' I demanded loudly.

'Appa, we think Amma is missing!' blurted Sarang even before a hi or anything.

'Did you try behind the door?' he said.

'Paaa, no jokes! We aren't playing hide-n-seek! She's been at a meeting all day, and we are still here at the Vittala temple complex, and she was to join us at five, and we just got a call from someone saying….'

Appa listened to the three of us, as we took turns to fill him in on the sparse details we had.

'Is Chandru there? Let me talk to him please,' said Appa.

We walked across to where Chandru was having an animated chat with a tourist. After talking to Appa for a bit, he gave the phone back to Nakul and said, 'Don't worry kids, I know everyone in Hampi. We'll find your mother in a jiffy. Let's go to the project office first. Maybe she's still in the meeting. Your father said some very, very important meeting. Ok?'

Appa spoke to us again. 'Oh kids, I wish I were there with you. But relax. Don't get all sleuthy, ok? Chandru has promised to help. Listen to him and call me if you hear anything.'

Chandranna asked us to follow him to his autorickshaw. Kaapi ran and jumped into the auto, waiting for us to catch up. The auto was very colourful, with its many flags fluttering in the wind. 'Best Guide in

Hampi' said one. Huddled inside the auto, we reviewed the situation. I pulled out my notebook and pencil.

What did we have so far?

- No call from Amma at lunch or after. uncharacteristic. Strange.
- If phone missing, why no msg or call directly from her on a borrowed mobile?
- Amma had said imp day. Why? For whom?
- That guy Bhupati looked mean. Suspicious.
- Must be a serious prob. Coz Appa did not crack any other dad-jokes after that first one.

As we poured over my scribbled list, Chandranna's auto rattled through the city. Once at the site office, we ran towards the main door. A young man was locking up.

'Suresha, *yelli pa ivaralla*?' Chandranna asked in Kannada.

'Bengaluru madam, Bhupati sir, and some other people left after lunch. No, no … after coffee, which they had immediately after lunch. Krishna drove them. Wait, I'll call him.' After talking animatedly on the phone for a few seconds, Suresha said, 'It seems Krishna took them to inspect several spots and then dropped your mother off at the hotel.'

'What? So, she just went back to the hotel and did not let us know?' Sarang wailed.

'Call the hotel, call the hotel. Call Amma again,' I yelled at Nakul.

He glared at me and tried her phone. Still dead. Then he called the guest house. The receptionist sounded sleepy.

'Brinda madam … let me see. I just came on this shift. Maybe, Ashwini will know … she's just finished her shift … umm—'

'—go to the room and find out now,' thundered Nakul, in his best police-officer *Singham* voice.

After a minute, the man said, 'Sir, there is a Do Not Disturb card on the door, and Ashwini told me madam was going to sleep because she had a headache. Anything else sir?'

We looked at each other stupidly.

'I told you to call the guest house when we first got that bogus call!' said Sarang.

'You didn't,' I countered.

'Let's go to the guest house,' said Chandranna.

Once at the guest house, Sarang was the first to disregard the Do Not Disturb card and barge into Amma's room.

'Sarang, hi, what's the time?'

'Ma, are you alright? What happened? Where were you? Why didn't you tell us yourself that you weren't feeling well?'

'Hey, hey, hey, mister, slow down, I already have a headache like I said on a message to Nakul—'

'You did not!'

'What?'

'Message.'

'Of course, I did. Look, here … oh, where's my phone?'

That part about the phone going missing was true, after all. We filled her in on the events of the day.

'Ok, ok, stop. My phone has all the notes I made today. And some videos too that I recorded that … uh, umm, no problem,' she tapered off. But we knew something was a problem—Amma was hiding something.

'C'mon Ma, what's the problem? Tell us,' I said, tugging her hand.

'It's just that … well, no, I did *not* leave my phone around for some monkey to conveniently walk away with it. And no, I did not tell anyone to call you … so who was that? And where is my phone now? I need it! It has….'

What did it have?

A Hush-Hush Project

1407, Vijayanagara

'What are you hiding there, Shubha?' said Raviraja.

'N-n-n-nothing!' said Shubha, trying to push away the parchment she had drawn on.

Shubha's cousin was just a year younger than her. Like his grandfather Guna, Raviraja was fond of travelling and meeting new people. Someday, he would become an important member of the court, wielding the power to govern and improve Vijayanagara, while she would be married off to a stranger. No one would even look at the designs she had worked on with her grandfather to make the city even greater.

Shubha had overheard rumours of people plotting against the king. Foolishly, she had written down their names, hoping to show the list to someone who could take it to the king. One of those names belonged to a man her grandfather trusted deeply, so she couldn't show it to him either.

'C'mon, show me what you have there? Is it another of your plans for the city?'

Shubha considered him for a moment. Could he be her ally? 'Actually, it's something to do with spoiling a plan.'

'What plan? Whose plan?'

'Do you know Muthuraju's nephew? The eldest one?' ventured Shubha.

'Kantharaj, the tall one who is always showing off his archery skills? He is—'

'—what?'

'Very bad, he is. I hope you never cross him,' said Ravi, his voice dropping to a whisper. 'Whenever he sees someone looking at him while he's outdoors, he will aim an arrow at some small bird in the royal garden and kill it. Just like that. Such a cruel boy.'

The royal gardens were renowned far and wide for the abundant greenery and the variety of birds that flocked there—peacocks, nightjars, bulbuls, and parakeets. Visitors from distant lands, aware of the king's refined tastes, often brought him exotic saplings and birds.

'Well, I overheard him speaking to a man I don't know. He—'

'—what were you doing near that bully?'

'I was sitting with my friends behind the jasmine bushes near the pond when I heard him. The boy was boasting that his uncle and a few others were planning to sabotage the new dam being built on the Tungabhadra. He claimed that any damage to the construction would be seen as a bad omen, and Deva Raya would abandon the project.'

'But why would they want to do it?'

'I don't know about that, but I believe they think that building the dam would take water away from their land. I know for sure that our thathagaru or our Raya would never go ahead with a project that involved robbing citizens of their share of water.'

'Hmm….'

'As a girl, I don't get to go out as much as you do, you lucky kid! But I've been observing and listening to rumours and doing my own sleuthing … look!' said Shubha, handing him the parchment paper.

'A list? Who are these people? Muthuraju's name is here too,' observed Raviraj.

'These are the men I believe are plotting something big. You see, all of them have land on the southern side of the city, which gets much less water than the north. They are planning to make a private canal by removing the rocks stacked up as part of the new dam and using them to block an existing canal. That way, they think they can divert more of the Tungabhadra to reach their land!'

'Are you sure?' said Ravi. 'What do we do now? Let's tell thathagaru.'

'No, no. He … he'll never believe that Muthuraju is going against the king. And he'll just scold us for getting into such things.'

'Then, what should we do? Just let them plot and get away with a crime?' said Ravi indignantly.

'Calm down, brother, calm down. If you really care for our kingdom, there is one thing you can do.' Shubha ran to close the heavy wooden door and whispered, 'Ravi, you often practice making state speeches with the king's son in a private chamber, don't you? And the king comes to watch his son? Can you—I know this is dangerous—can you find the right moment when no one is around but you and the king—no ministers, servants, family, no one!—and slip him the list without a word? Don't tell your friend about it either. Only the king must know about it. And don't tell the king about me. Is that possible?'

Shubha scribbled a few more details against each name. She had drawn a map to show the river and the new dam. She had also marked the direction of the water flow and the private land around it. She took a minute to take in all that she had written, and then with a deep sigh, she handed it over to her cousin. 'God bless you, Raviraj, may no harm come to you or the kingdom, ever. Take care.'

Just then, they heard their thathagaru walking in. 'Quick, hide it,' said Shubha.

'Already in,' confirmed Ravi, patting the inside of his coat as he snuck away through the side door.

Seekers at the Station

What would you like to do today?' said Amma at breakfast.

For what it was worth, she had filed a missing phone complaint on the official police website. She told the receptionist at the hotel too, just in case a kind soul found the phone and called in.

'Very doubtful, Madam,' said the receptionist. 'Monkeys would have taken it and just broken it. Hampi people are good, not too many robbers. But monkeys! Costly phone, Madam?'

'Not expensive, but very precious….'

'Oh, sir must have given it to you for your birthday,' said the beaming lady, likely having heard countless tales of Vijayanagara kings gifting their wives precious jewels. Chandranna had even mentioned how the rulers would send elephant loads of gifts to damsels in other kingdoms to show their interest in marriage.

'Hmm … actually, my children bought it for me,' said Amma. Our family wasn't great at gifting. For my last birthday, my parents got me a natural clay water bottle while my friend Umaima got a swimming pool. Yes, a real pool—not membership to a pool. With a new apartment attached to it. In the centre of one of Bengaluru's poshest localities. And the family moved there too. In our family, we usually celebrate a birthday by ordering in food if it is a weekday, or driving to some place on the outskirts of the city if the date falls on a weekend. The phone we got for Amma was a huge deal for us. We had to pool our pocket money to get a simple one for her because my dear brother Sarang was foolish enough to push Amma's off the table while playing football. Inside the house. Which he was not supposed to do obviously! Silly fellow.

Now, he was kicking me under the table.

'What?' I mimed. Lost in my thoughts while also munching on the *akki* roti and chutney, I had no idea what the family was discussing. Sarang jerked his head to draw my attention to what Amma was saying.

'I have to go to the water board in a bit for a meeting. Would you like to go to school?'

'School? Why? Where? What for?' he said incredulously.

'To learn, of course! The Outdoor School Project has some openings for volunteers today. You can help local kids do some nature sketching or public speaking. In turn, they can teach you about the local birds, plants, and folklore. Starts at two, after the primary school kids finish their regular classes. You could stay here till lunch time and then go to Vidyaniketana, or, you could visit the archaeological museum right across the road, come back for lunch, and then go to the school.'

Nakul looked at me. Then, both of us looked at Sarang. He gave an excited little nod.

'What's with that look?' Amma said, raising her eyebrows.

'Look? What look? Hey, Devi and Nakul, do you think we should sign up for it?' Sarang said.

'Ok, that sounds better than sitting here all day,' I said with a sigh so exaggerated that Nakul later remarked my mother would have surely suspected we were up to something behind her back.

'What better way to get out of the guest house and try to get back Brimma's phone,' Nakul said in a low voice once we were alone again.

The Seekers, it seems, were facing their first case in many months. Would they be able to solve it?

After Amma left, we quickly discussed what we should and could do. 'We have to visit the police station and tell someone about the phone. No use depending on that online complaint Amma has registered. Who takes online complaints seriously anyway?' I said.

'And they'll take complaints from a couple of kids and a teenager seriously?' scoffed Nakul.

'Of course, they'll listen to us,' Sarang said confidently. 'We'll present the case properly. I'm sure the police will help. The Indian police system is the best!'

Sarang's class had recently visited a police station in Bengaluru as part of their excursion to study safety in the city. He had been totally floored by the DGP's talk. It seems Ms Tarangini had shown them the offices, fancy cyber systems, and talked about the work they did to crack crimes.

We looked at each other.

'We can tell them about Amma's work. As much as we know about it. And we should definitely tell them about Bhupati. I'm sure he has something to do with the disappearance of her phone,' I said.

'But we can't tell the police everything! I mean, what if the police officer is Bhupati's friend?' said Nakul.

'Of course we have to give them all the information we have! Ms Tarangini told us how police officers go by facts and their findings. They don't show any partiality towards family and friends.'

'You've not seen many cop movies, kids! Grow up,' said Nakul.

Finally, we decided to do things calmly. First, visit the police station. Next, ask to talk to someone in charge of thefts. Then, follow our instinct—see if we feel we can trust the person, and then tell them as much as we can.

We got ready to go to the police station down the road. It was the most impressive police station I had ever seen. Built to replicate elements of the Hampi monuments, the building made a pretty picture against the boulders and greenery. It was cool inside, even though we were all feeling pretty nervous.

'So, you've come to report a missing mobile phone? Hmm … were there any monkeys around when this happened?' asked SP Anupama Ashwin.

'We don't now, but my mother would never leave her phone around so that a monkey could pick it up,' I said.

'But our Hampi monkeys are very smart, you know,' the police officer said proudly.

'But Amma is smarter,' blurted Sarang.

After a few more casual questions, Nakul could not hold it in any longer.

'Ma'am, I believe my aunt has very sensitive information related to her work on her phone, and we suspect that someone she knows might have taken it,' Nakul said in a rush. The inspector closed the door, returned to her seat and said, 'And who do you suspect, and why?' All caution went flying out the window as we took turns to tell her everything we knew about the situation. She was impressed

that Nakul had the traffic app and listened to us keenly.

'Now that we have a lot of information, why don't you let us do our jobs. I'll let you know if something comes up.'

Why Is Shubha Called?

1407, Anegundi

Shubha waited impatiently to hear something from Raviraj. Had he managed to pass on the list to the king? Had the king seen it? Would he believe her? 'My dear princess, who are you waiting for? Expecting someone special? I think you've run to the door at least a hundred times today?' asked her grandfather.

'Nothing like that, Thathagaru. My friends had sent word that they may come in a day or two so we can try out our new clothes for the festival,' Shubha blabbered.

The old man knew that wasn't the truth. His granddaughter had never shown any interest in clothes. But he was wise enough to know when he must leave a teenager alone. 'I'll rest for a while, my princess. May god bless you.'

But even before he could go to his chamber, there was a knock on the door. Shubha rushed to open it. When she saw who was at the door, her face went pale.

'Who is it?' asked her grandfather.

'Namaskara Vijendra *avare*! We have come bearing a message from Satyavathi Devi *avaru*. She wants to meet your granddaughter. May we proceed, please?'

Shubha was certain her grandfather could see her trembling. She wondered if the guards could see it too.

'Aah! Of course, of course!' said the old man. 'It must be about the proposal … umm … nothing, nothing. Shubha, go on, go listen to what Satyavathi *avaru* has to say.'

Why was the wife of a minister calling her? Had she caught Raviraj trying to talk to the king? Where was Raviraj? Why hadn't he come to see her? Shubha was sweating profusely now. Or, that is how she felt. Years of training to appear graceful in any situation helped her now to maintain some dignity. She fell at her grandfather's feet, took his blessings, and walked with her held high behind the guards. She had done no wrong. If she were to be punished for something she had done with the kingdom's best interest at heart, so be it. Once outside the safety of her home, Shubha wondered if it was very foolish to have meddled with something she had no business in. After all, she knew that Srimathi Satyavathi and Muthuraju were cousins. Close cousins.

A drop of cold sweat trickled down her neck.

Case Closed ... Too Soon

Pleased with the outcome of our visit to the police station, we trudged on to the Hampi Archaeological Museum. 'Oh, look here! All of Hampi's most important monuments represented in this model. We went here, and here … and there!' said Sarang, pointing to the replica of the city. It showed the river and canals too. Now that we had a sort of bird's-eye view of the entire area, I understood why Amma was so excited about anything to do with Hampi.

Nakul looked around to check for any boards prohibiting photography. Not seeing one, he happily started clicking pictures of the exhibits. 'Here is the Bukka Aqueduct that Mahi showed us! Oh, and can you believe that—'

Nakul's phone rang.

'Who is it? Who?' barked Nakul.

'Is that Amma?'

'It's Mahi,' whispered Nakul.

'Why're you whispering, silly? Talk to him,' I said.

'Hello? Hello? Hello, is that Mahi?'

The call dropped.

'I'm pretty sure that was Mahi. I think he sounded anxious. Or excited. Or … maybe nervous?'

'Do you think we should call him back?'

Ting ting.

I grabbed Nakul's phone and read the incoming message. It was clearly written by someone in a hurry.

Cometo Kala niketan if want see yashkhgna rehersall 3pn. Pl pl cme.

The next message had the location.

We decided to have lunch at a restaurant instead of returning to the guest house. Nakul texted Amma on her temporary number that we were going to watch a yakshagana performance at Ranga Mandira instead of going to the school to volunteer. Just as we were getting into an auto, Amma called. Nakul listened to her, nodded several times, and then said sheepishly, 'Yes,

Breema, we knew you had registered a complaint, but we saw this beautiful police station and felt like visiting it. So … umm … since we were there, we decided to make sure they were acting on your complaint.'

Liar! But sometimes lying for a cause is allowed, right?

Then, after more vigorous nodding into the mobile—as though Amma could actually see him through the phone!—he rang off. 'Guess what, they found Brimma's phone! From a petty thief. She has spoken to SP Anupama, and we have to go and pick it up from the station now.'

We rushed to the station but had to wait for some time before we were let into the SP's room.

'So, children, here is the mobile phone. Give it to Dr Brinda. Someone seems to have wiped it clean. Factory reset,' she informed us.

This meant all of Amma's notes and photos and videos would have gone!

'How did you get it so quickly?' said Sarang, his eyes shining.

'I can't tell you everything, but we caught an old man trying to sell a phone to a group of young tourists and took him in for questioning. He said he just needed some money to go home to his daughter's house because his son was ill-treating him.'

'How horrible,' said Nakul. 'Imagine children doing this to their own parents.' His face was getting red. This always happened to him when it was about a parent being ill-treated.

'Who would have thought that Mahi could do this! And he had told me his father was in Mysore,' murmured the SP. 'Oh sorry, sorry, I was just feeling bad that someone I thought I could trust turned out to be the villain. Now, run along children, enjoy your stay in Hampi.'

'Did you say … Mahi?' said Nakul, his voice down to a whisper.

'Mahi … Mahayuti? Who works with Ambara Constructions?' I added quickly.

'Yes, you know him?'

'He is a member of the group our mother is working with. We met him a couple of days back.'

'Oh, hmm … I had always liked him. He's so proud of Hampi and the local art and culture. Now I don't know what to think,' said the SP with a sigh and sent us on our way.

How foolish of us to not tell the SP that it was, in fact, Mahi who had invited us to the yakshagana performance!

'Let's tell Amma everything,' said Sarang.

'No, let's go to the auditorium,' countered Nakul. 'We'll be careful about what we tell Mahi if we meet him. We have to find the connection between him, the theft, and the work Brimma is doing,' explained Nakul.

One part of me agreed with Sarang, while the other was drawn to Nakul's idea. The thrill of seeking answers won, and we proceeded to the auditorium.

A Secret Passage

1407, Anegundi

Shubha followed the guards through a dark corridor and reached a quiet courtyard filled with plants. Bulbuls and parakeets flew in and out of the green cover. Satyavathi Devi called her in, and they settled down on the edge of a small pool. The guards moved away respectfully, leaving the two women together. Shubha's heart was beating so fast that she was sure the queen could hear it thumping in her chest. Was this the calm before the storm? Was this when the queen would offer her a poisoned drink? Shubha had heard stories about sons killing their own fathers to get to the throne.

'I hear you like to draw,' said the queen.

Taken by surprise, Shubha stuttered, 'Huh? Oh, oh yes, yes, I love to draw.' But how did she know?

'I saw what you sent to the king. It was very well presented.'

Shubha waited. Did the queen mean her handwriting or the contents of the parchment?

'I need someone whom I can trust. The king and my husband are very busy. I want to help them. Deva Raya *avare* showed me the list of people who you think are conspiring to commit acts against the kingdom. He has already initiated a plan to check your suspicions. I think you are wrong about my cousin. Look, I'm telling you this in secret because I think you're good at keeping secrets. I believe your grandfather does not know about the list you passed on to Raviraj? Muthuraju is actually working undercover, to find out about the people trying to break the dam. I love him dearly, and I'm sure he is innocent. But if you are right, and he is planning to do something wrong, then I'll be the first to have him punished!'

Shubha seemed to have been holding her breath for too long. Now, she let it all out and came closer to the queen. 'Please tell me how I can help.'

What the queen said next sent a thrill up Shubha's spine.

'I called you because I have an idea for a building just for women and children. Not for the royal ladies—they already have a lovely enclosure—but for women and children like you and me. Where we can gather and exchange ideas about the state. We can discuss politics and our land, our rivers, our fields. And the children can have a safe place to play peacefully nearby. I have the ideas, but I need someone to put those ideas in the form of drawings. Would you like to do it?'

Shubha was so stunned that she could only nod her head vigorously.

'Once it is ready, we will present it to the king and the ministers. So, it has to be our secret till then. Agreed?'

Shubha couldn't believe her eyes! How wonderful that she was being asked to help with something especially meaningful for the women and girls of Vijayanagara!

'You'll have to come here regularly for some days. But what will you tell your grandfather? Hmm … you can tell him that I have commissioned you to….'

Shubha gathered her skirt and ran out of the courtyard. The guards were waiting at a distance. They escorted her respectfully back to her house. Thathagaru was waiting for her eagerly.

'What did Satyavathi Devi have to say to you?'

'Er ... she wants me to make a ... portrait of her,' she lied, just like Satyavathi Devi had hinted. 'Someone told her that I draw well. So, I'll have to go to her royal chamber every day for the next few days.'

This was probably the first time that she was consciously lying to her dear grandfather. It was also the first time Shubha felt truly thrilled to be doing something in secret. Like her grandfather, she too had always wanted to be part of something special to make Vijayanagara even better.

Yakshagana

A young lady was waiting at the door of the auditorium. As soon as she saw us, she opened the door and ushered us in, asking us to take the third row from the stage. There were only a few other spectators. A senior man was up front directing the actors. 'Ok, start, Valli enters … and action!'

The loud music, colourful clothes, and starkly painted faces of the actors drew us right into the play. Nakul got into the act by interpreting the dance-drama for us.

'This is the famous fight between the Vanara brothers, the monkey-king Vali and his brother, Sugriva. Vali does not want his brother to help—'

'—stop, Naks. Thank you but we too know this bit about the *Ramayana*,' I said and concentrated on the action on stage.

Vali and Sugriva twirled and jumped and encircled each other with so much energy that it was difficult to tell who was who. Just when Vali jumped high on the stage, trying to pounce on Sugriva, an arrow zipped through the stage and hit him on his back. With an anguished cry, Vali slumped to the floor, leading to a round of applause from the audience.

In the *Ramayana*, the battle between the Vanara brothers takes place in Kishkinda. Kala Niketan's production was also scheduled to be performed at Kishkinda, the town we now know as Anegundi. How much more dramatic could it be to watch a yakshagana performance on an outdoor stage, set against the hills and boulders of Anegundi—the first capital of the Vijayanagara kingdom!

The actor playing Vali got up, walked to the edge of the stage, and asked the director, 'All ok, Sir?'

Something in the way he talked seemed familiar.

'That's Mahi,' whispered Sarang.

'How right that he is playing the cruel Vali,' said Nakul.

Mahi peered into the audience and spotted us immediately. He waved a hand that seemed to say, 'come over to the side'.

'Let's get out, fast,' I said, pulling the boys towards the door.

'No, let's go speak to him. What can he do to us in front of so many people?' the boys chimed in together.

'What if there's no one with him?' I said.

'Scaredy cat! Come!'

Reluctantly, I followed the boys to the green room. Mahi was waiting for us, and he quickly pulled Nakul towards him.

'Come, come, kids, did you like the show?'

His face looked even scarier from up close. The thick black-and-white winged strokes around his eyes and the red and green paint made his face seem large and demon-like. 'So, you got the phone from the police station?' he said slowly and deliberately as he wiped his face with oil.

We stood like statues. How did he know that?

'And everything on the phone was deleted?'

'We don't know anything. Amma just asked us to go and pick up her phone from the station,' said Sarang.

'And did the SP tell you about my father? And how I ill-treated him?'

We looked at each other wildly. What were we supposed to say? His face looked quite ugly now with the colours all mixed up and smeared on his face.

'Look, I don't want to waste time explaining things but SP Anupama called me a few hours ago.' Then, he pulled out another phone from a pouch and said, 'Here, take this phone. It has all the information that was on your mother's phone.'

For once, all three of us were tongue-tied.

'Yes, I got it from—' Spotting the musicians walking towards the green room, he added quickly, 'Kids, act like you are student reporters or autograph seekers or something, and you don't know me personally.'

'So, Sir, is yakshagana popular in Hampi?' asked Nakul sharply, with his phone extended towards Mahi as though he was recording the artist.

The musicians left their instruments on a table and left. We let out a collective sigh.

'My father is a farmer in Mysore. That man who stole your mother's phone is related to us, but he does not live with me. And, he is a good man too ... and a good gardener. He is not a thief. He does odd jobs in many houses in Hampi and Hospet. But sometimes, when he is a little drunk, his personality changes completely. I'm sure someone got him to steal your mother's phone and lie to the police. I think I know who it is … and why.'

'Who?' Sarang said wide-eyed.

'Shhh … later. Once I know for sure. Now, don't tell anyone that I gave you this phone. Give it to your mother at the earliest. And tell her to leave for Bengaluru as soon as possible. And if there is any problem at all, please ask her to get in touch with me or Bhupati. Best of luck!'

Sugriva and Hanuman walked in. Mahi gestured for us to leave.

'Do you believe Mahi?' Sarang whispered as we started to rush out. 'Why is he wishing us good luck?' he muttered through clenched teeth. 'What does he think is going to happen to us?'

Mahi came running to us a few minutes later. By now, he had wiped off all the paint from his face. 'Run! Go back quickly. And stay safe, ok? Don't go around snooping in police stations and other places!'

We slipped out as fast as we could and headed to the nearest autorickshaw stand.

'Hey, wait,' said Nakul, taking out the phone and placing it on a rock outside the building. 'How can we trust him? How do we know that this … this … this phone is not a sleeper cell or something?'

Almost involuntarily we stepped back a few feet from the phone. It rang. We jumped back further. It stopped ringing. Nothing happened. I took a deep breath and gave in to my gut feeling. 'Guys, you know what, I think Mahi meant what he said. I think we should trust him. Let's take this to Amma.'

***

Amma was back in the guest house by the time we returned.

We trooped into her room.

'Brimma, here's your phone,' said Nakul, with a flourish.

'Thanks, kids. You know it's a very special phone. I've been so….'

Was that a tear that I saw in her eyes? Totally uncharacteristic!

'Ma, what's wrong?' I said.

'Nothing, nothing. I'm just glad you're back. It's been a rough day.' She was looking into the phone as she muttered under her breath, 'Of course, there is nothing in it. Everything has been deleted.'

'Don't you back up everything on the cloud, Mom? You should, you know,' said Sarang, in a voice that felt like *he* was the adult in the room. 'How could you have been so foolish!'

'That's enough, young man! Of course I back up my stuff on cloud. But this time, the storage was full, the network was patchy … and now some very sensitive information is lost,' she lamented.

'Try this,' said Nakul, giving her Mahi's phone.

'What's this? Who gave this to you?' Amma hastily switched on the phone and peered into it. Then with a yelp, 'Oh … Mahi! My saviour! And it seems to have all my material! Thanks, kids,' she added with a smile.

'Amma, what's all this? What's going on? Strange things have been happening all week. You can tell us … we're not kids,' I said as calmly and dad-like as possible.

'Shall we order room service? Some snacks and early dinner right here in my room?' said Amma.

Yes, that sounded good.

The Spy Who Came to Hampi

'Ok, I'm sorry I haven't shared everything with you, and anyway, I can't,' said Amma, once we'd all settled on her bed. 'But here's the gist of it. Remember I told you that this project I've been working on for the past few months is about reviewing a new tourism infrastructure plan and my role in it as a water resource specialist? Well, the project involves state and private parties. The rules for building new structures in a UNESCO Heritage Site are quite tough. The locals are fighting against the proposed tourism plan. Not against the development of hotels, roads and other infrastructure, but against the kind of buildings and plans being made, and the places suggested for them.'

'You mean, the locals don't want tourists? Or, new hotels for tourists?'

'No, no, tourists are most welcome. And good hotels too. But the locals want to know if they can welcome tourists into their own homes. They want to cook and serve local food to visitors. They want to be trained as guides. Their children are going to school and learning many languages. Just like you. So, they want their children to learn from visitors about the world beyond these boulders. And they want to continue with their farming practices. The Gangavathi taluk near Hampi is called the rice bowl of Karnataka, you know. There are also many artisans here who know how to use local materials like seeds and banana fibre to make beautiful objects. My friends want them to be given opportunities to earn their livelihood.'

'Chandranna was telling us how, in the Vijayanagara kingdom, foreigners used to come and stay with people. How everyone learnt from each other,' said Sarang in his best good-boy voice.

'But all these rulers also went to war against each other, and kept wanting more and more and more,' I added, suddenly disgusted at how wars were happening even in today's world.

'Out of context,' said Nakul loudly. 'What has that got to do with what Brimma is saying?'

'All connected,' I argued. 'We have to learn from history and aim for a better future, isn't it? Not repeat the same things like war, war, war!' I burst out.

'Hey, hey, kids, I'm telling the story here! I think someone here is hangry!' said Amma.

On cue, there was a knock on the door. Nakul let in the waiter who came bearing fries and pakodas. As we dug into the snacks with generous amounts of ketchup, Amma went on with her story.

'But along with it, there's another agenda too. An undercover one.'

'Oh my god, Ma, are you a spy? Like a real spy? Carrying a little gun and all that?'

'Of course not, Sarang! C'mon!'

'Oh,' said Sarang, a bit disappointed that his mother was just a non-spy like all the other people he knew.

'And if I were a spy, I wouldn't tell you that, would I?' teased Amma. Was she being serious? Was my mother a spy? 'Seriously, no. No, I'm not a spy working for the CBI or RAW or anything like that. I'm part of a network of organizations that work on similar projects—or rather, we all believe in conserving natural resources. Organizations like Water Wisdom, Otter Conservation Society, Save Our Crocodiles, Oota Koota, and Mahi's group called Kishkinda Artisan Collective. You see, we do need hotels, roads, bridges, buildings, and tourist kiosks. But we also need local communities and local wisdom to thrive. We believe that governments can do this without driving out villagers and their wisdom.'

'But what is your role here? And why is someone wanting to push us down the Tungabhadra, or steal your phone?' I asked.

'No one tried to push us down the river….'

'But, the other day, Bhupati lied to you about the roadblock! He deliberately wanted us to take the coracle,' pointed out Nakul.

'Oh, poor man. He just wanted to make sure I saw and documented the riverbank conservation work that he and his group have been doing. They are letting local plants grow freely along the banks and experimenting with other suitable ones like vetiver grass. Plants that hold soil and stop the banks from eroding. And Bhupati wanted to make sure I remembered to include the people whose lives depended on coracles for their livelihood.'

'What? Bhupati is a good guy?' I asked, unwilling to believe what my mother was saying.

'He's a very committed Hampi conservationist. He and young Mahi too,' she added with a smile.

'Then who's the villain?'

'It's … I don't know yet. And even if I knew, what sort of a spy would I be if I told you everything?'

'Come on, you're not really a spy,' we groaned together.

'How can you be sure of that?' asked Amma very softly.

That stumped us for just a second.

'Hey, you *can't* be a spy,' said Sarang, exasperated.

'Ma, you didn't complete what you were saying … what's your role in this whole side business?' I said.

'Hoi, not side business! Our conviction, you could say. I've been chosen by the network to file this document and submit it to the authorities. We want the government to show prudence and modify the proposed tourism plan.'

'And someone does not want you to do that?' asked Nakul.

'Yes. And they know—and we don't yet know how—that I recorded some very strong voices from the community in our favour.'

Another knock. Dinner was served. Joladda rotti, banana flower curry, plain rice, and curd. The food was the tastiest I'd had in a long time.

Amma's phone rang. After finishing the call, she said calmly, 'Kids, get your things together, we're leaving for Bengaluru tonight instead of tomorrow. Something's come up. And … don't tell anyone about it.'

'Now? We're leaving a day earlier? And you're telling us now?' I protested.

'No time to explain. That was Bhupati on the phone. He is arranging for the tickets. Unfortunately, Krishna can't come in the car since his mother is in the hospital. Chandru is going to pick us up in half hour.'

'Yay, we get to see Kaapi again,' I said.

'But how will we all fit into an auto?' asked Sarang.

'It will be a squeeze, yes. But better that than going with a stranger who may knock off Brimma's … umm … laptop with all its secrets, right Ms Spy?' teased Nakul.

Amma wasn't smiling. 'Something like that. So … ok, now, run up boys!'

'You *are* a spy!' exclaimed Sarang.

Within an hour, we were on the train. Amma quickly set up her berth and prepared to lie down. 'I'm going to sleep right away. Dead tired. And tomorrow is going to be a really busy day,' she said. 'You had all better stretch out quickly too. Our train arrives in Bengaluru at 5.30 in the morning. I've set my alarm, ok?'

Just as the train pulled out of the platform, I caught a glimpse of a man jumping into the moving train. And it looked like he was getting into our bogie. Something about him was familiar. 'That's Krishnanna,' I whispered. 'What's he doing here?'

'Definitely not looking after his mother in a hospital,' said Nakul.

'Amma, amma,' I whispered. But she was fast asleep.

'Maybe he's just come to say bye to mom and us,' reasoned Sarang. 'Or maybe he's not even coming towards us. And it may not even be him.'

'Doubt that! Are you thinking what I am thinking, Dee-dee? He's our villain! And he's back to steal Brimma's phone or laptop for sure!'

'Definitely looks like that. Remember what we did in Patan? Operation Repeat? Ready?'

'And if he's not the villain then no harm done, ok, Sarang?' I pacified him.

Quick as a wink, we drew the curtains, removed amma's laptop and phone from her bag and kept them away near the far end of the seat, and switched off the lights. Nakul had his head out from the curtain, just a little, to see if it was indeed Krishna, and if he was really coming to us. We placed Amma's almost empty bag strategically near the aisle, so that it was visible to anyone walking down the aisle. Then we waited. Sarang fished out the whistle he always carried with him ever since the incident in Patan. Nakul was set, ready to stick his leg out at the right moment. After what seemed like an eternity, we saw a hand slide in through the slightly open curtain and snatch the bag. Almost instantly Sarang started blowing hard on the whistle. I switched on the lights, and Nakul put his foot out. Krishna tripped. 'Thief! Thief!' we shouted. The Seekers had got the man! The other passengers helped restrain Krishna. The commotion had woken up the passengers around as well. Someone summoned the ticket inspector who came within minutes and thanked us for being vigilant. 'These thieves! Worse than monkeys,' he muttered.

'What happened?' asked Amma, rubbing her eyes.

'Ammaaa, you're definitely *not* a spy,' declared Sarang firmly, before proceeding to fill her in.

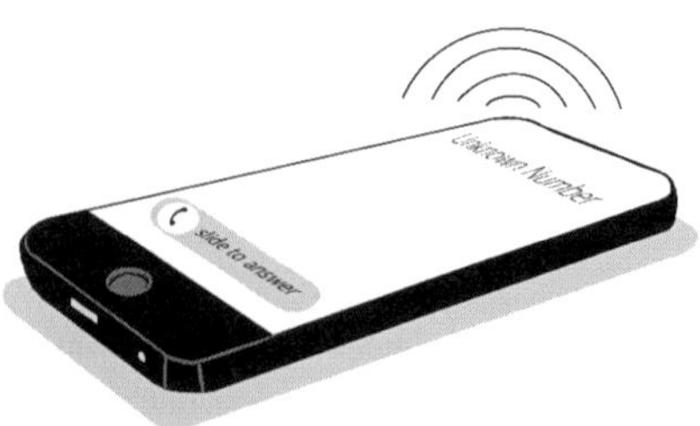

At the next station, two policemen came in and took Krishnanna away.

Back Home

When the train reached Bengaluru, Appa was at the station to pick us up. 'So glad to see you all back hale and hearty,' he said.

It seemed like we hadn't seen him for ages. Never had we been so communicative so early in the morning! There was so much to tell him! Appa had to keep saying, 'wait, wait, say that again' because we were all talking together. In our excitement of having caught not just a thief but also a conspirator, we'd forgotten that Appa too had just got back from a trip.

'Appa, how was your trip?'

'Lovely! The students were very fit and enthusiastic. The weather was perfect. And I, as always, was delighted to be in the mountains!'

Amma got working as soon as she had freshened up. Sarang and Nakul went back to sleep and only got up for brunch. Now that I was back home, I couldn't wait to call my bestie and classmate Suhana to catch up on all the news in Bengaluru.

'What news? You've only been away three days!'

'Really?'

'Oh, yes, but there is some news. Your parents must have got an email too. We have to go to school tomorrow to pick up whatever things we'd left there.'

Appa was unpacking. He took out a few things and went to his glass cabinet. 'Look at this beautiful stone, a feldspar gneiss with a touch of garnet. Found it on the road near Namik glacier. It will always remind me of—'

'—your awesome trip to Namik valley?' I asked.

'No, actually it will always remind me of you all. I had it in my hand when you spoke to me on the phone from Hampi. When you said somebody was going to push you into the water, remember? At that minute, all I wanted was for you all to be safe, and for us to be together. In that second, I realized I would have happily thrown away this beautiful stone, and every last one in my precious collection if it meant I could ensure your safety.'

That was quite a speech! Too much, and I think we both realized that simultaneously. We weren't really a family that said such things to each other, you know. I wanted to tell him about the missing Hampi stone but suddenly I felt a big lump rise up my throat. Seriously, how could I talk to him then?

The next morning, we went to school in a rickety auto. The ground was still wet in patches around the school. We walked carefully and went into the lobby. Tables had been set up all around, with the classes written on a placard. Deepa ma'am was at our table. 'C'mon, students, stop jostling, come one by one, and pick up whatever belongs to you,' she said.

Each table had a small queue. 6B had the longest. But, of course! Pens, pencils, water bottles, notebooks, textbooks—all stacked on the table. My heart sank. Who would think of saving a little stone? Oh, there was my chunky pencil box that I'd forgotten about. It was in this that I'd taken the rock. I opened it quickly and … no rock.

UDAYA HIGH SCHOOL
ಉದಯ ಪ್ರೌಢಶಾಲೆ

'If any of you want to pick up your paintings, it's on that other table,' said Deepa ma'am, pointing to the one hidden behind her. And there, holding down all the sheets of paper was a lovely paperweight. The D-rock! In a swift action, I swooped down on the little rock and slid it into my pencil box. Now, all I had to do was wait for Sarang and Nakul to get their things.

Back home, I was going to put the rock back quietly. Then, I thought of what Appa had said this morning. It was only right that I told him what I had done. And just when I cleared my mind, squared my shoulders, and gathered my courage—goodness, so much work—the brat spoke up.

'Appa, Appa, do you know what Dee-Dee did with your rock?' announced Sarang. I aimed the rock at him before handing it quickly to Appa. My voice cracked several times as I narrated the whole story about the missing rock of Hampi. But when I finished, Appa simply gave me an awkward hug. No scolding or harsh words. He never does that.

Turning the stone as though it were the Kohinoor, Appa said, 'Beautiful, isn't it? Do you know why I like geology so much? It's because rocks can tell things as they happened, when they happened. They can tell us a lot about the location too. Understanding a rock's composition helps identify the best places to dig wells, make canals and lakes … understanding land is so important.'

'Like the planners of Vijayanagara did,' I said.

It struck me suddenly that geology is a lot like history. Both are mostly about the past. Both hold solutions for present-day problems. And both can be used for a better future.

'Hey boys, I think I know the answer to a question that most adults ask us when they meet us for the first time: what do you want to be when you grow up? Well, I'm going to be a historian! No, a landscape designer! No, no—'

'I'm going to … not decide anything now,' said Nakul.

'I'm going to be a spy,' said Sarang happily.

Our brand-new Udaya High School reopened on January 26, 2025. It was such a joy to cycle to school again and park our bikes in the old cycle stand—now straightened and painted, of course. The brick-red-and-yellow exterior of the building looked awesome.

Our classroom was the best. Newly polished wooden desks and chairs, a big new smartboard, a water station, and even a reading nook. A perfect place to park the book that I'd finally finished reading, *Shubha's Victory in Vijayanagara.*

Canals, Culprits, and Visionaries

1407, Anegundi

It had been ten days since Shubha finished drawing the pool and play area that Satyavathi Devi had described. Ten days since Satyavathi Devi had shown the drawing to the king. Ten days since the time Shubha felt like something would burst inside her if she did not tell her grandfather the truth about how she had made a list of people whom she suspected of harming the kingdom.

Just as she fixed a long strand of jasmine flowers in her hair, her grandfather came in. 'I'm going to be very busy over the next few days,' he said. 'Raya has given me a new project. I have to get the construction started immediately.'

His voice seemed strange. He seemed angry. And nervous. And, he also seemed to be very sad.

'Thathagaru, what is it? You seem unhappy. Is it something you do not want to build?'

'No, no! In fact, it is something I'll be very happy to build. It is one of the sweetest designs I have seen so far. But…'

He sighed deeply. 'We found out today that a few rocks had been dislodged from the dam that we are building. We were shocked to find the missing rocks piled up at the mouth of an important canal. People I know and have trusted were trying to break the dam. Muthuraju was—'

Wham! Shubha felt like someone had pelted a stone at her. Her heart sank. So, Satyavathi's cousin was a villain after all!

'—able to catch the culprits red-handed. He is a fine young man indeed.'

'You mean, Muthuraju is a good man?'

'He is. But why do you ask?'

Shubha took a deep breath. She looked down for a minute, then looked up straight into her grandfather's eyes and said, 'Thathagaru, I have kept some things secret from you. I was the one who suspected that these men were planning to damage the dam.' The floodgates opened, and Shubha rushed to tell him about the things she had overheard, her list and Raviraj's help, and about Satyavathi Devi's promise to take the matter to the king.

'Oh, my dear child, you don't know what a dangerous thing you were doing! If they were ready to go against the king, can you imagine how much they could hurt you, a child? I can't lose you … you're most precious to me!'

'I'm sorry, Thathagaru. And I have another confession to make. You see, Satyavathi Devi did not summon me to paint her portrait. She asked me to help her with her plan and—'

'Aha, about that I know everything! And that is the plan I have been asked to follow and build. What a beautiful park it is going to be for the women and children of Vijayanagara. Was that water slide for children your idea? What a clever way to make the same water go up a channel and down through another into the little pool!'

Shubha blushed with pride and pleasure. Praise from one of the greatest engineers of Vijayanagara—the one who had built so many anicuts and canals!

Epilogue

Amma is busy working—openly!—on a proposal that involves rainwater, lakes, wells, and recycled water. It's Bengaluru, 2025, and the city is still grappling with its water future. 'If done well, this water can fill up a thousand lakes! Everyone will have water for drinking and other needs, including water for livelihoods like fishing and farming,' she has been saying. She's really excited. Oh, and guess what? Amma got a call from SP Anupama. The brothers who own Ambara Constructions are now in jail with Krishnanna for trying to sabotage Amma's work! Mystery solved!

Appa has been looking longingly at a rock in his shelf; he says it is from an oil-field in Arunachal Pradesh. Will his next trek be to Patkai hills, I wonder.

And, as for me, of course, I had to do a project on water for the Annual Science Festival.

Water Is Life

If you've been near a natural water body—a river, lake, or beach—you know what a treat it is for all our senses. And how do you feel when you see a glass of clean water after coming in, sweating, from a game? Ah, the best drink in the world! Now, imagine if you had to put in a lot of effort just to get that glass of water. Ouch!

While most people in urban India have clean water on tap, the price we pay for it as a nation is very high. City administrations spend enormous amounts to supply water to their citizens, either by extracting it from deep underground or transporting it from distant rivers.

Ancient civilizations had ingenious ways of tapping into natural resources. For instance, over half a million people in the old city of Hampi, during the Vijayanagara empire, thrived despite receiving very little rainfall. How? Because they studied the land and understood it. They let nature do its job. This knowledge helped them build a water system with trenches and pits in the hillsides to collect rainwater and channel it towards wells in strategic locations.

Water is one of the most precious resources on earth. If we adopt best practices from both the past and present, we can ensure enough water for everyone. By learning from history and understanding our current challenges, we can work towards a healthier and happier future for all.

What do you spot?

Hampi was the capital of the Vijayanagara empire from 1336 to 1565. During this time, many travellers visited the city and wrote about its beauty. The most famous chronicles are those of the Persian scholar Abd-al-Razzaq Samarqandi, the Portuguese traveller Domingo Paes, and the Venetian merchant Niccolò

dé Conti. They described the riches of the bazaar and the grandeur of the temples and palaces.

Now, it's your turn to observe this artistic representation of the Hampi bazaar during the Vijayanagara empire. Turn back this page—can you spot the different animals, the various activities, the diverse dressing styles, and the fabulous wares on sale?

Cool Systems of Hampi

A group of monuments at Hampi was declared a UNESCO World Heritage Site in 1986. Many of the monuments are in ruins but are being preserved. Here are some features marked on a map. The city had an excellent water supply system, some parts of which are still functioning today. Dive in, and take a look at a part of Devyani's school project on water management.

Water Systems of Hampi

Anjanadri Hills
Anegundi
Tungabhadra River
Vijaya Vittala Temple
Pushkarni
Octagonal Bath
Stone Trough
Water Canal
Kalyani
Queens' Bath

Bukka's aqueduct

Photo credits: Mala Kumar

This 200-metre stone structure once carried water from Anegundi canal to Virupapur Gaddi. Now in ruins.

Raised water channels

Photo credits: Wikimedia Commons

These stone trough carried water acros rocky terrain into beautifully crafted tanks called kalyani or pushkarini.

negundi anicut

he Anegundi anicut,

reserved by locals,

howcases Vijayanagara's

ngineering, diverting

iverwater without modern concrete.

Photo credits: Sudarshan Varma

Restored stepwell

Photo credits: Mohan S. Rao

A pushkarini is a stepped water tank, often built near temples. This pushkarini in Hampi was restored by the ASI in 2007.

Acknowledgments

I never imagined, during my daydreams in history class, that I would one day write a book based on history. Yet here I am, immersed in reading, researching, and writing about it. For this, I am grateful to the incredible work of historians, archaeologists, and all those who bring history to life.

To write this book, I spoke with many individuals from progressive organizations dedicated to sustainability, heritage conservation, and natural resource management—each grounding their work in the needs of both present and future generations. Then, I did something a little sneaky—I borrowed bits of their characteristics, blended them together, and created entirely new, imaginary people. These composite characters became the heart of this book!

Now, let me introduce you to the real heroes:

Founder of the Rainwater Club and trustee of Biome Environmental Trust, Vishwanath S. has, through his columns, talks, and photographic records of traditional wells, made a compelling case for sustainable solutions to ensure water for all.

Landscape architect and environmental design consultant Mohan S. Rao worked with the Archaeological Survey of India to restore an ancient *pushkarini* in the Vitthala Temple complex in Hampi. He generously shared his time and documents with me.

Founder of The Kishkinda Trust, convenor of INTACH Anegundi, and artist, Shama Pawar welcomed me into an idyllic world on the banks of the Tungabhadra, where art, culture, and livelihoods thrive alongside traditional agriculture. Her work since 1996 to empower the local community and promote sustainable tourism is nothing short of a miracle.

Dr Chitra Krishnan has written extensively on the merits of traditional irrigation systems. Talking to her about anicuts and other water elements was not only informative but also reinforced the idea that learning from history is far more important than merely learning about it.

President of the Water Users' Cooperative Society of Anegundi, Sudarshan Varma spoke to me about the land, the farmers, and their hopes of being part of sustainable, just, and practical conservation solutions for the region. His resistance to concretizing the Anegundi anicut has helped preserve and showcase a remarkable feat of historical engineering.

INTACH Bengaluru and its convenor, Meera Iyer, worked to restore Fort High School, which inspired the charming little school in this story.

The work of Arghyam and the India Water Portal has kept me grounded in the reality that water can never be taken for granted.

This book would never have taken shape without Anuradha Srinivasan, a member of FIHCR's YUVA wing. Along with Rasika Bhale and the team at FIHCR, she kept me going on this historical journey.

Illustrator Megha Vishwanath was a joy to work with. With her talent, meticulous research, and professionalism, we couldn't have asked for a better collaborator.

Arpita Dasgupta quietly edited my draft and gave invaluable suggestions, while the team at BluOne Ink gave me the freedom to work at my own pace.

That the young SPIC MACAY volunteer I met as a journalist decades ago would one day become a prolific author, historian, and founder of FIHCR is amazing. Vikram, thank you for unknowingly leading me to the serene banks of the Tungabhadra, where Purandaradasa composed his songs so many centuries ago. I will cherish those moments forever.

And to Kumar, who took me to Hampi years ago when I had just regained my legs after a near-fatal accident—and again recently for this book—thank you! But brace yourself … the next book may take us much farther from home!

To Rishi, the young reader, thank you! Your thumbs up on the blind draft was most reassuring!

And dear reader, thank you for picking up this book!

About the Author

Mala Kumar is a children's book author and editor based in Bengaluru. Her books include *Travelling Treasures: 100 Incredible Tales of How Things Came to India, Up the Mountains of India, Crazy Mazy's Maths Puzzles*, and over 40 picture books including the *Ritu Chakra* series and a biography of Sir M. Visvesvaraya. She writes about education, culture, environment, and people for different publications.